CASEY AT THE BAT

AND OTHER POEMS TO PERFORM

Editor MARJORIE L. BURNS
Designer MARIJKA KOSTIW
Cover Illustrator PETER CATALANOTTO

ISBN 0-590-35614-3

12 11 10 9 8 7 6 5 4   3/9

ACKNOWLEDGMENTS

Grateful acknowledgment is made to the following authors and publishers for the use of copyrighted materials. Every effort has been made to obtain permission to use previously published material. Any errors or omissions are unintentional.

ABP International for "The Flattered Flying Fish" from THE FLATTERED FLYING FISH AND OTHER POEMS by E. V. Rieu. Reprinted by permission of Michael Rieu, son and executor of the Estate of E. V. Rieu.

Constable and Co., Ltd. for "Oath of Friendship" from Arthur Waley's CHINESE POEMS. Reprinted by permission of Constable Publishers.

Doubleday for excerpts from HOMER, THE ODYSSEY, translated by Robert Fitzgerald. Copyright © 1961 by Robert Fitzgerald. Reprinted by permission of Doubleday, a division of Bantam Doubleday Dell Publishing Group, Inc.

Editions Gallimard for "The Stars" translated by Jerome Rothenberg from Preyre's French version as printed in Caillois and Lambert, TRESOR DE LA POESIE UNIVERSELLE. Copyright 1958 by Editions Gallimard.

Farrar, Straus & Giroux, Inc. for "A Sick Child" from THE COMPLETE POEMS by Randall Jarrell. Copyright © 1949 and renewal copyright © 1976 by Mrs. Randall Jarrell. Reprinted by permission of Farrar, Straus & Giroux, Inc.

Benjamin E. Haller for "The Ups and Downs of the Elevator Car" by Caroline C. Emerson. Reprinted by permission of Benjamin E. Haller, Executor, Estate of Caroline C. Emerson.

Harcourt Brace Jovanovich, Inc. for "Arithmetic" from THE COMPLETE POEMS OF CARL SANDBURG, copyright 1950 by Carl Sandburg and renewed 1978 by Margaret Sandburg, Helga Sandburg Crile and Janet Sandburg, reprinted by permission of Harcourt Brace Jovanovich, Inc.; and for "Tall Tales," abridged from "#45" in THE PEOPLE, YES by Carl Sandburg, copyright 1936 by Harcourt Brace Jovanovich, Inc. and renewed 1964 by Carl Sandburg, reprinted by permission of the. publisher.

Morton L. Leavy for nine poems from SPOON RIVER ANTHOLOGY by Edgar Lee Masters. Copyright 1915, 1916, 1942, and 1944 by Edgar Lee Masters. For "Achilles Deatheridge" from THE GREAT VALLEY by Edgar Lee Masters. Copyright 1917 by Edgar Lee Masters. Reprinted by permission of Morton L. Leavy, attorney for the Estate of Edgar Lee Masters.

Random House, Inc. for "Oath of Friendship" from TRANSLATIONS FROM THE CHINESE, translated by Arthur Waley. Reprinted by permission of Alfred A. Knopf, Inc.

CONTENTS

INTRODUCTION

If you're like the majority of people, you will never be a professional actor, let alone a famous star of stage or screen. But that doesn't mean you can never have the fun of performing before an audience. You can have it if you wish—and without trying out for a role in a play. All you need to do is get together with friends and take part in a dramatic reading.

You might like to start your career by performing one of the dramatic readings in this book. Each is a poem (or group of related poems) that has been arranged for reading by two or more persons. Some are narrative poems with dialogue; these give you a chance to describe the action (if you are the narrator) or to portray a character. Others are lyrical or humorous poems that challenge you to create a mood or provoke laughter. All the poems, however, have one thing in common: they depend for their effect on your voice and the voices of your fellow performers.

You don't have to have a "beautiful" speaking voice to succeed as a dramatic reader. However, you do need to be able to speak loudly and distinctly enough to make yourself heard. In addition, you need to have a certain amount of control over the tone, pitch, and volume of your voice, so you can project an emotion or attitude appropriate to the words you are speaking. This kind of interpretive reading increases the audience's appreciation of the poem and makes your performance more enjoyable both for them and for you.

This poem first appeared in the regular column that Ernest Lawrence Thayer wrote for a San Francisco newspaper. It was made famous by DeWolf Hopper, a comedian who recited it hundreds of times in theaters across the country. The humor of the poem lies in its mock seriousness: It makes a baseball game in Mudville sound like an event of earth-shaking importance.

CASEY AT THE BAT

ERNEST LAWRENCE THAYER

SPEAKERS

NARRATOR 1	ONE FAN
NARRATOR 2	FANS
CASEY	ECHO
UMPIRE	

NARRATOR 1

The outlook wasn't brilliant for the Mudville nine that
    day;
The score stood two to four with just one inning left to
    play.
And so, when Cooney died at first and Burrows did the
    same,
A sickly silence fell upon the patrons of the game.
A straggling few got up to go in deep despair. The rest
Clung to the hope that springs eternal in the human
    breast;
They thought

FANS

If only Casey could but get a whack at that—
We'd put up even money now, with Casey at the bat.

NARRATOR 2

But Flynn preceded Casey, as did also Jimmy Blake,

And the former was a no-good and the latter was a fake;
So upon that stricken multitude grim melancholy sat,
For there seemed but little chance of Casey's getting to
    the bat.
But Flynn let drive a single, to the wonderment of all,
And Blake, the much despisèd, tore the cover off the
    ball.
And when the dust had lifted, and they saw what had
    occurred,
There was Jimmy safe at second and Flynn a-hugging
    third.

NARRATOR 1

Then from the gladdened multitude went up a joyous
    yell;
It rumbled in the mountaintops, it rattled in the dell;
It struck upon the hillside and rebounded on the flat,
For Casey, mighty Casey, was advancing to the bat.
There was ease in Casey's manner as he stepped into his
    place;
There was pride in Casey's bearing and a smile on
    Casey's face.
And when, responding to the cheers, he lightly doffed
    his hat,
No stranger in the crowd could doubt 'twas Casey at the
    bat.

NARRATOR 2

Ten thousand eyes were on him as he rubbed his hands
    with dirt;
Five thousand tongues applauded when he wiped them
    on his shirt.
Then while the writhing pitcher ground the ball into
    his hip,
Defiance gleamed in Casey's eye, a sneer curled Casey's
    lip.

And now the leather-covered sphere came hurtling
    through the air,
And Casey stood a-watching it in haughty grandeur
    there.
Close by the sturdy batsman the ball unheeded sped—

CASEY

That ain't my style

NARRATOR 2

said Casey.

UMPIRE

Strike one!

NARRATOR 2

the umpire said.

NARRATOR 1

Then from the benches, black with people, went up a
    muffled roar,
Like the beating of the storm waves on a stern and
    distant shore.

ONE FAN

Kill him! Kill the umpire!

NARRATOR 1

shouted someone in the stands;
And it's likely they'd have killed him, had not Casey
    raised his hand.
With a smile of Christian charity great Casey's visage
    shone;
He stilled the rising tumult; he bade the game go on.
He signaled to the pitcher, and once more the spheroid
    flew;
But Casey still ignored it, and the umpire said,

UMPIRE

Strike two!

FANS

Fraud!

NARRATOR 2

cried the maddened thousands, and the echo answered

ECHO

Fraud!

NARRATOR 2

But one scornful look from Casey and the audience was
awed.

They saw his face grow stern and cold, they saw his
muscles strain,

And they knew that Casey wouldn't let that ball go by
again.

The sneer is gone from Casey's lips, his teeth are
clenched in hate;

He pounds with cruel violence his bat upon the plate.

And now the pitcher holds the ball, and now he lets it
go,

And now the air is shattered by the force of Casey's
blow.

NARRATORS 1 AND 2

Oh, somewhere in this favored land the sun is shining
bright;

Somewhere bands are playing, somewhere hearts are
light,

Somewhere men are laughing, somewhere children
shout;

Ah, but there is no joy in Mudville—mighty Casey has
struck out!

This poem is like a series of nesting boxes. The first stanza starts with a large, all-inclusive unit, "the kingdom." Next it moves to a smaller unit within the kingdom (a city), then to a town within the city, and so on down to a tiny unit within all the others: a basket of flowers. The second stanza moves in the opposite direction, from small to large. Listeners will be more likely to perceive the poem's formal structure if they hear the lines read by nine different voices. All speakers should maintain a steady, chant-like rhythm.

THIS IS THE KEY

ANONYMOUS

SPEAKERS

SPEAKER 1	SPEAKER 6
SPEAKER 2	SPEAKER 7
SPEAKER 3	SPEAKER 8
SPEAKER 4	SPEAKER 9
SPEAKER 5	

ALL SPEAKERS

This is the Key of the Kingdom:

SPEAKER 1

In that Kingdom is a city;

SPEAKER 2

In that city is a town;

SPEAKER 3

In that town there is a street;

SPEAKER 4

In that street there winds a lane;

SPEAKER 5

In that lane there is a yard;

SPEAKER 6

In that yard there is a house;

SPEAKER 7

In that house there waits a room;

SPEAKER 8

In that room an empty bed;

SPEAKER 9

And on that bed a basket—

ALL SPEAKERS

Of Flowers, of Flowers;
A basket of Sweet Flowers.
(Pause. Then continue more rapidly, in a singsong tone.)
Flowers in a Basket;

SPEAKER 9

Basket on the bed;

SPEAKER 8

Bed in the chamber;

SPEAKER 7

Chamber in the house;

SPEAKER 6

House in the weedy yard;

SPEAKER 5

Yard in the winding lane;

SPEAKER 4

Lane in the broad street;

SPEAKER 3

Street in the high town;

SPEAKER 2

Town in the city;

SPEAKER 1

City in the Kingdom—

(Pause.)

ALL SPEAKERS

(Slowly and deliberately.)
This is the Key of the Kingdom;
Of the Kingdom this is the Key.

The poems on these three pages are taken from one of Shakespeare's best-loved comedies, *As You Like It*. The first speaker is a duke who has been driven from his lands by his unscrupulous brother and who is living in exile in the Forest of Arden. Jaques and Amiens are two noble courtiers who are sharing the duke's banishment. Jaques' years of involvement in court politics have given him a rather sour view of life and human nature. Amiens, although also disillusioned, is less cynical than Jaques. To add drama to Jaques' speech, you might have seven people mime (act out silently) the seven stages of a man's life as Jaques describes them.

LINES FROM *AS YOU LIKE IT*

WILLIAM SHAKESPEARE

SPEAKERS

DUKE	AMIENS
JAQUES	

DUKE

We are not all alone unhappy:
This wide and universal theater
Presents more woeful pageants than the scene
Wherein we play.

JAQUES

All the world's a stage,
And all the men and women merely players:
They have their exits and their entrances,
And one man in his time plays many parts,
His acts being seven ages. At first the infant,
Mewling[1] and puking in the nurse's arms.
And then the whining school-boy, with his satchel
And shining morning face, creeping like snail
Unwillingly to school. And then the lover,

Sighing like furnace, with a woeful ballad
Made to his mistress' eyebrow. Then a soldier,
Full of strange oaths, and bearded like the pard,[2]
Jealous in honor, sudden and quick in quarrel,
Seeking the bubble reputation
Even in the cannon's mouth. And then the justice,
In fair round belly with good capon lined,[3]
With eyes severe and beard of formal cut,
Full of wise saws and modern instances;[4]
And so he plays his part. The sixth age shifts
Into the lean and slippered pantaloon,[5]
With spectacles on nose and pouch on side,
His youthful hose, well saved, a world too wide
For his shrunk shank; and his big manly voice,
Turning again toward childish treble, pipes
And whistles in his sound. Last scene of all,
That ends this strange eventful history,
Is second childishness and mere oblivion,[6]
Sans[7] teeth, sans eyes, sans taste, sans everything.

DUKE

Give us some music; and, good cousin, sing.

AMIENS

Blow, blow, thou winter wind.
Thou art not so unkind
As man's ingratitude;
Thy tooth is not so keen,
Because thou art not seen,
Although thy breath be rude.
Heigh-ho! sing, heigh-ho! unto the green holly:
Most friendship is feigning,[8] most loving mere folly.

DUKE, JAQUES, AND AMIENS

Then, heigh-ho, the holly!
This life is most jolly.

AMIENS

Freeze, freeze, thou bitter sky,
That dost not bite so nigh
As benefits forgot:
Though thou the waters warp,
Thy sting is not so sharp
As friend remembered not.
Heigh-ho! sing, heigh-ho! unto the green holly:
Most friendship is feigning, most loving mere folly.

DUKE, JAQUES, AND AMIENS

Then, heigh-ho, the holly!
This life is most jolly.

[1] **mewling:** whimpering

[2] **pard:** leopard

[3] **belly with good capon lined:** Jaques is referring to the practice of bribing judges with gifts of poultry.

[4] **wise saws and modern instances:** trite old sayings and examples of how they apply to modern life

[5] **pantaloon:** dotard. The word derives from the name of a stock character in Italian comedy, Pantaleone, a foolish old man whose costume includes slippers and tight trousers and stockings.

[6] **oblivion:** forgetfulness

[7] **sans:** without

[8] **feigning:** pretending

THE TIDE RISES, THE TIDE FALLS

HENRY WADSWORTH LONGFELLOW

SPEAKERS

SPEAKER 1	CHORUS
SPEAKER 2	SPEAKER 4
SPEAKER 3	

SPEAKER 1

The tide rises, the tide falls.

SPEAKER 2

The twilight darkens, the curlew calls;

SPEAKER 3

Along the sea-sands damp and brown
The traveler hastens toward the town,

CHORUS

And the tide rises, the tide falls.

SPEAKER 2

Darkness settles on roofs and walls,

SPEAKER 1

But the sea, the sea in the darkness calls;

SPEAKER 4

The little waves, with their soft, white hands,
Efface the footprints in the sands,

CHORUS

And the tide rises, the tide falls.

SPEAKER 3

The morning breaks; the steeds in their stalls
Stamp and neigh, as the hostler calls;
The day returns,

SPEAKER 4

but nevermore
Returns the traveler to the shore,

CHORUS

And the tide rises, the tide falls.

The king in this old ballad is John of England, who reigned from 1199 to 1216. John was unpopular with practically everybody, including the Pope, who excommunicated him, and his barons, who in 1215 forced him to sign the Magna Carta (Great Charter), the first English bill of rights. The author of the ballad portrays John as cruel and treacherous, but does give him credit for having a sense of humor. The second character in the story is an abbot (head of a monastery) who is too rich and splendid for his own good. The third character, a humble shepherd, turns out to be the cleverest and the wisest of the three.

THE KING, THE ABBOT, AND THE SHEPHERD

ANONYMOUS

SPEAKERS

NARRATOR	ABBOT
KING	SHEPHERD

NARRATOR

An ancient story I'll tell you anon,
Of a notable prince, that was called King John;
He ruled over England with main and might,
But he did great wrong, and maintained little right.
And I'll tell you a story, a story so merry,
Concerning the Abbot of Canterbury;
How for his housekeeping and high renown,
They rode post to bring him to London town.
A hundred men, as the king heard say,
The abbot kept in his house every day;
And fifty gold chains, without any doubt,
In velvet coats waited the abbot about.

KING

How now, Father Abbot? I hear it of you,

That you keep a far better house than I do;
And for your rich living and high renown,
I believe you work treason against my crown.

ABBOT

My sovereign Liege, I would like it known,
I am spending nothing but what is my own;
And I trust your Grace will not put me in fear,
For spending my own true-gotten gear.

KING

Yes, yes, Father Abbot, your fault is high,
And now for the same you'll have to die;
And unless you can answer me questions three,
Your head struck off from your body shall be.
Now the first question: As I sit here,
With my crown of gold on my head so fair,
Among all my liegemen of noble birth,
You must tell to one penny what I am worth.
Secondly, tell me, beyond all doubt,
How quick I may ride the whole world about;
And at the third you must not shrink,
But tell me here truly, what do I think?

ABBOT

These are deep questions for my shallow wit,
And I cannot answer your Grace as yet;
But if you will give me a fortnight's space,
I'll do my endeavor to answer your Grace.

KING

Now a fortnight's space to you will I give,
And that is the longest you have to live;
For unless you answer my questions three,
Your life and your lands are forfeit to me.

NARRATOR

Away rode the abbot, all sad at this word,
To the colleges at Cambridge and Oxenford;
But not one professor was there so wise
That he could by his learning an answer devise.
Then home rode the abbot, with comfort cold,
And he met his shepherd, a-going to fold.

SHEPHERD

Now, good Lord Abbot, you are welcome home;
What news do you bring us from King John?

ABBOT

Sad news, sad news, Shepherd, I must give:
That I have but three days more to live.
I must answer the king his questions three,
Or my head struck off from my body shall be.
The first is to tell him as he sits there,
With his crown of gold on his head so fair,
Among all his liegemen of noble birth,
To within one penny, what he is worth.
The second, to tell him, beyond all doubt,
How quick he may ride this whole world about;
And at question the third I must not shrink,
But tell him here truly, what does he think?

SHEPHERD

Cheer up, my Lord; did you never hear yet
That a fool may teach a wise man wit?
Lend me your serving-men, horse, and apparel,
And I'll go to London to answer your quarrel.
With your pardon, it oft has been told to me
That I'm like your lordship as ever can be,
And if you will but lend me your gown,
There is none shall know us at London town.

ABBOT

Now horses and serving-men you shall have,
With sumptuous raiment gallant and brave;
With miter and staff and all symbols you need
To make you look like an abbot indeed.

KING

Now welcome, Sir Abbot, and welcome, I say;
'Tis well you've come back to keep your day;
For if you can answer my questions three,
Your life and your living both saved shall be.
And first, as you see me sitting here,
With my crown of gold on my head so fair,
Among my liegemen of noble birth,
Tell to one penny what I am worth.

SHEPHERD

For thirty pennies Jesus was sold
By Judas Iscariot, as I am told;
And twenty-nine is the worth of thee,
For I think thou art one penny worse than He.

NARRATOR

The king he laughed, and swore by Saint Bittle:

KING

I did not think I was worth so little!
Now secondly tell me, beyond all doubt,
How quick I may ride this world about.

SHEPHERD

Rise with the sun, and ride with the same,
Until the next morning he rises again;
And then your Grace need never doubt
But in twenty-four hours you'll ride it about.

NARRATOR

The king he laughed, and swore by Saint Joan:

KING

I did not think I could do it so soon!
Now from the third you must not shrink,
But tell me truly, what do I think?

SHEPHERD

That I shall do, and make your Grace merry:
You think I'm the Abbot of Canterbury.
But I'm his poor shepherd, as you may see,
Come to beg pardon for him and for me.

NARRATOR

The king he laughed, and swore by the mass:

KING

I'll make you abbot today in his place!

SHEPHERD

No, no, my Liege, be not in such speed;
For alas! I can neither write nor read.

KING

Four gold coins a week, then, I'll give to thee,
For this merry jest you have shown to me;
And tell the abbot, when you get home,
That you've brought a free pardon from good King
John.

Here's a possible "stage" arrangement for this poem: The Elevator Man, in an imaginary elevator car, stands facing the audience. The Narrator stands on one side of the imaginary elevator door, and the Chorus stands farther away on the other side. The person who speaks the words of the Elevator Car might be seated behind the Elevator Man.

THE UPS AND DOWNS
OF THE ELEVATOR CAR

CAROLINE C. EMERSON

SPEAKERS

NARRATOR	ELEVATOR MAN
ELEVATOR CAR	CHORUS

NARRATOR

The elevator car in the elevator shaft,
(presses button to call elevator)
Complained of the buzzer, complained of the draft.
It said it felt carsick as it rose and fell,
It said it had a headache from the ringing of the bell.

ELEVATOR CAR

There is spring in the air,

NARRATOR

sighed the elevator car.
Said the elevator man,

ELEVATOR MAN

You are well-off where you are.

CHORUS

The car paid no attention but frowned an ugly frown
                              when
                    up   it
                going   should
          started   be
     it   going
And   down.

*(During the next few lines the Narrator becomes more and
    more excited and keeps pressing the button.)*

NARRATOR

Down flashed the signal, but *up* went the car.
The elevator man cried,

ELEVATOR MAN

You are going much too far!

NARRATOR

Said the elevator car,

ELEVATOR CAR

I'm doing no such thing.
I'm through with buzzers buzzing. I'm looking for the
     spring.

NARRATOR

Then the elevator man began to shout and call

CHORUS

And all the people came running through the hall.

NARRATOR

The elevator man began to call and shout,

ELEVATOR MAN

The car won't stop! Let me out! Let me out!

NARRATOR

On went the car past the penthouse door.
On went the car up one flight more.
On went the elevator till it came to the top.
On went the elevator, and it would not stop!

CHORUS

Right through the roof went the man and the car.
And nobody knows where the two of them are!
(Nobody knows but everyone cares,
(Chorus members pretend to climb stairs.)
Wearily, drearily climbing the stairs!)

NARRATOR

Now on a summer evening when you see a shooting
    star
Fly through the air, perhaps it *is*—that elevator car!

Of the characters in this poem, only the child is real; the others
are figments of the child's imagination. To make it clear to the
audience that the words of the postman and the visitors from
outer space are coming from the child's mind, the people who
play these roles might be seated behind the one who plays the
child. Of course it's part of the child's game to pretend that the
postman is standing nearby and that the visitors have just landed
their spaceship outside in the yard.

A SICK CHILD

RANDALL JARRELL

SPEAKERS

CHILD   POSTMAN
VISITORS FROM OUTER SPACE

CHILD

> The postman comes when I am still in bed.
> "Postman, what do you have for me today?"
> I say to him. (But really I'm in bed.)
> Then he says—what shall I have him say?

POSTMAN

> This letter says that you are president
> Of—this word here; it's a republic.

CHILD

> Tell them I can't answer right away.

POSTMAN

> It's your duty.

CHILD

> No, I'd rather just be sick.
> Then he tells me there are letters saying everything
> That I can think of that I want for them to say.

I say, "Well, thank you very much. Good-bye."
He is ashamed, and turns and walks away.
If I can think of it, it isn't what I want.
I want . . . I want a ship from some near star
To land in the yard, and beings to come out
And think to me:

VISITORS FROM OUTER SPACE

So this is where you are!
Come.

CHILD

Except that they won't do,
I thought of them . . . And yet somewhere there must be
Something that's different from everything.
All that I've never thought of—think of me!

The lines on these pages are taken from a longer poem called "The People, Yes," in which Carl Sandburg celebrates the energy, endurance, and good humor of the American people. In the "Tall Tales" section he includes some of the humorous exaggerations and outright lies that Americans have been laughing at for generations. The jokes seem to fall into four groups: a series of short ones introduced by the opening statement "They have yarns"; the listeners' reactions to the jokes ("baloney," said in a variety of funny ways); some fairly long anecdotes; and another series of short jokes linked by the word "nor." The performers of this poem should react to each other's lines. They should also be ready to pause for laughter from the audience.

TALL TALES

CARL SANDBURG

SPEAKERS

NARRATOR 1	LISTENER 1	SAILOR
BARN-SHINGLER	LISTENER 2	VOICES
NARRATOR 2	LISTENER 3	TWO CHEATERS
SHEEP COUNTER	LISTENER 4	ROBERT TOOMBS
JOHN HENRY	RAFFLE WINNER	

NARRATOR 1

    They have yarns
    Of a skyscraper so tall they had to put hinges
    On the two top stories so to let the moon go by,
    Of one corn crop in Missouri when the roots
    Went so deep and drew off so much water
    The Mississippi riverbed that year was dry,
    Of pancakes so thin they had only one side,
    Of a fog so thick

BARN-SHINGLER

    we shingled the barn and six feet out on the fog

NARRATOR 2

Of Pecos Pete straddling a cyclone in Texas and riding it
   to the west coast where it rained out under him,
Of the old man's whiskers:

NARRATOR 1

When the wind was with him his whiskers arrived a
   day before he did

NARRATOR 2

Of the ship captain's shadow: it froze to the deck one
   cold winter night,
Of the sheep counter who was fast and accurate:

SHEEP COUNTER

I just count their feet and divide by four

NARRATOR 1

Of the man so tall he must climb a ladder to shave
   himself,
Of the hook-and-eye snake unlocking itself into forty
   pieces, each piece two inches long, then in nine
   seconds flat snapping itself together again,
Of horned snakes, hoop snakes, that roll themselves
   where they want to go, and rattlesnakes carrying
   bells instead of rattles on their tails

NARRATOR 2

Of the herd of cattle in California getting lost in a giant
   redwood tree that had hollowed out,
Of the man who killed a snake by putting its tail in its
   mouth so that it swallowed itself,
Of railroad trains whizzing along so fast they reach the
   station before the whistle,

NARRATOR 1

Of Paul Bunyan's big blue ox, Babe, measuring between

the eyes forty-two ax-handles and a plug of Star
tobacco exactly,
Of John Henry's hammer and the curve of its swing and
his singing of it as

JOHN HENRY

a rainbow round my shoulder.

LISTENER 1

Do tell!

LISTENER 2

I want to know!

LISTENER 3

You don't say so!

LISTENER 4

For the land's sake!

LISTENER 2

Gosh all fish-hooks!

LISTENER 1

Tell me some more.
I don't believe a word you say
but I love to listen
to your sweet harmonica
to your chin-music.

LISTENER 3

Your fish stories hang together
when they're just a pack of lies:
you ought to have a leather medal:
you ought to have a statue
carved of butter: you deserve
a large bouquet of turnips.

RAFFLE WINNER

The number 42 will win this raffle, that's my number.

NARRATOR 2

And when he won they asked him whether he guessed the number or had a system. He said he had a system:

RAFFLE WINNER

I took up the old family album and there on page 7 was my grandfather and grandmother both on page 7. I said to myself this is easy for 7 times 7 is the number that will win and 7 times 7 is 42.

NARRATOR 1

Once a shipwrecked sailor caught hold of a stateroom door and floated for hours till friendly hands from out of the darkness threw him a rope. And he called across the night:

SAILOR

What country is this?

NARRATOR 1

and hearing voices answer

VOICES

New Jersey

NARRATOR 1

he took a fresh hold on the floating stateroom door and called back half-wearily

SAILOR

I guess I'll float a little farther.

NARRATOR 2

When the Masonic Temple in Chicago was the tallest

building in the United States west of New York, two men who would cheat the eyes out of you if you gave 'em a chance, took an Iowa farmer to the top of the building and asked him,

TWO CHEATERS

How is this for high?

NARRATOR 2

They told him that for $25 they would go down in the basement and turn the building around on its turn-table for him while he stood on the roof and saw how this seventh wonder of the world worked. He handed them $25. They went. He waited. They never came back.

This is told in Chicago as a folk tale, the same as the legend of Mrs. O'Leary's cow kicking over the barn lamp that started the Chicago fire, when the Georgia visitor, Robert Toombs, telegraphed an Atlanta crony:

ROBERT TOOMBS

Chicago is on fire, the whole city burning down, God be praised!

NARRATOR 1

Nor is the prize sleeper Rip Van Winkle and his scolding wife forgotten, nor the headless horseman scooting through Sleepy Hollow

NARRATOR 2

Nor the sunken treasure-ships in coves and harbors, the hideouts of gold and silver sought by Coronado, nor the Flying Dutchman rounding the Cape doomed to nevermore pound his ear nor ever again take a snooze for himself

NARRATOR 1

Nor Jim Liverpool, the riverman who could jump
across any river and back without touching land
he was that quick on his feet

NARRATOR 2

Nor the man so lean he threw no shadow: six
rattlesnakes struck at him at one time and every
one missed him.

Sidney Lanier was an eminent musician as well as a poet. In fact, during his career with the Peabody Symphony Orchestra of Baltimore, he was considered by many the greatest flute player in the world. Lanier believed that it was possible to create a kind of music out of words, and this poem is one of his most successful attempts to do so. In it, we hear the rushing waters of the Chattahoochee River, which rises in the hills of northern Georgia and flows southward for 410 miles to Lake Seminole. Along the way, plants, rocks, and trees tempt the river to linger; but it knows that its duty is to water the plain, and it hurries on.

SONG OF THE CHATTAHOOCHEE

SIDNEY LANIER

SPEAKERS

CHORUS	**SPEAKER 3**	**SPEAKER 6**
SPEAKER 1	**SPEAKER 4**	**SPEAKER 7**
SPEAKER 2	**SPEAKER 5**	

CHORUS

Out of the hills of Habersham,
Down the valleys of Hall,

SPEAKER 1

I hurry amain[1] to reach the plain,
Run the rapid and leap the fall,
Split at the rock and together again,
Accept my bed, or narrow or wide,
And flee from folly on every side
With a lover's pain to attain the plain
Far from the hills of Habersham,
Far from the valleys of Hall.

CHORUS

All down the hills of Habersham,
All through the valleys of Hall,

SPEAKER 2

The rushes cried, *Abide, abide,*

SPEAKER 3

The willful waterweeds held me thrall,[2]

SPEAKER 4

The laving[3] laurel turned my tide,

SPEAKER 5

The ferns and the fondling grass said, *Stay,*

SPEAKER 6

The dewberry dipped for to work delay,

SPEAKER 7

And the little reeds sighed, *Abide, abide,*
Here in the hills of Habersham,
Here in the valleys of Hall.

CHORUS

High o'er the hills of Habersham,
Veiling the valleys of Hall,

SPEAKER 3

The hickory told me manifold
Fair tales of shade, the poplar tall
Wrought me her shadowy self to hold,

SPEAKER 6

The chestnut, the oak, the walnut, the pine,
Overleaning, with flickering meaning and sign,
Said, *Pass not, so cold, these manifold*
Deep shades of the hills of Habersham,
These glades in the valleys of Hall.

CHORUS

And oft in the hills of Habersham,
And oft in the valleys of Hall,

SPEAKER 4

The white quartz shone, and the smooth brook-stone
Did bar me of passage with friendly brawl,

SPEAKER 5

And many a luminous[4] jewel tone
—Crystals clear or a-cloud with mist,
Ruby, garnet, and amethyst—
Made lures[5] with the lights of streaming stone
In the clefts of the hills of Habersham,
In the beds of the valleys of Hall.

CHORUS

But oh, not the hills of Habersham,
And oh, not the valleys of Hall
Avail:[6]

SPEAKER 1

I am fain[7] for to water the plain.
Downward the voices of Duty call—
Downward, to toil and be mixed with the main.[8]
The dry fields burn, and the mills are to turn,
And a myriad[9] flowers mortally yearn,

CHORUS

And the lordly main from beyond the plain
Calls o'er the hills of Habersham,
Calls through the valleys of Hall.

---

[1] **amain:** at full speed [2] **thrall:** prisoner [3] **laving:** bathing

[4] **luminous:** shining [5] **lures:** things that attract or entice

[6] **avail:** have use or effect [7] **fain:** inclined, willing

[8] **main:** the sea. The stretch of river that flows from Lake Seminole to the Gulf of Mexico has a different name: Apalachicola.

[9] **myriad:** extremely great number

Like Sidney Lanier, Edgar Allan Poe wrote poems that seem made to be sung. In fact, "The Bells" is actually sung on occasion, for it has been set to music for mixed chorus. Although you will be speaking, not singing, the poem, you can make it sound musical by controlling the pitch, volume, and tone of your voice, and by speeding up and slowing down as the mood dictates. Four kinds of bells are described: silver, golden, brass, and iron. Each of these has its own distinctive sound and is associated with a certain event in life: a sleigh ride; a wedding; a disastrous fire; a funeral. Try to pronounce the words very clearly, especially words such as *tinkle, jingling,* and *clang* that imitate the sounds of the bells.

THE BELLS

EDGAR ALLAN POE

SPEAKERS

SPEAKER 1	**SPEAKER 4**
SPEAKER 2	**BELLS**
SPEAKER 3	

SPEAKER 1

Hear the sledges with the bells—

BELLS

Silver bells!

SPEAKER 1

What a world of merriment their melody foretells!
How they

BELLS

tinkle, tinkle, tinkle,

SPEAKER 1

In the icy air of night!

While the stars, that oversprinkle
All the heavens, seem to twinkle
With a crystalline delight;
Keeping time, time, time,
In a sort of Runic rhyme,[1]
To the tintinnabulation[2] that so musically wells
From the

BELLS

bells, bells, bells, bells,
Bells, bells, bells—

SPEAKER 1

From the jingling and the tinkling of the bells.

SPEAKER 2

Hear the mellow wedding bells—

BELLS

Golden bells!

SPEAKER 2

What a world of happiness their harmony foretells!
Through the balmy air of night
How they ring out their delight!—
From the molten-golden notes,
And all in tune,
What a liquid ditty floats
To the turtle-dove that listens, while she gloats
On the moon!
Oh, from out the sounding cells,
What a gush of euphony[3] voluminously[4] wells!
How it swells!
How it dwells
On the Future!—how it tells
Of the rapture that impels
To the swinging and the ringing
Of the

BELLS

bells, bells, bells—
Of the bells, bells, bells, bells,
Bells, bells, bells—

SPEAKER 2

To the rhyming and the chiming of the bells!

SPEAKER 3

Hear the loud alarum bells—

BELLS

Brazen bells!

SPEAKER 3

What a tale of terror, now, their turbulency[5] tells!
In the startled ear of night
How they scream out their affright!
Too much horrified to speak,
They can only

BELLS

shriek, shriek,

SPEAKER 3

Out of tune,
In a clamorous appealing to the mercy of the fire,
In a mad expostulation[6] with the deaf and frantic fire,
Leaping higher, higher, higher,
With a desperate desire,
And a resolute endeavor
Now—now to sit, or never,
By the side of the pale-faced moon.
Oh, the bells, bells, bells!
What a tale their terror tells
Of Despair!
How they

BELLS

clang, and clash, and roar!

SPEAKER 3

What a horror they outpour
On the bosom of the palpitating[7] air!
Yet the ear, it fully knows,

BELLS

By the twanging,
And the clanging,

SPEAKER 3

How the danger ebbs and flows;
Yet the ear distinctly tells,

BELLS

In the jangling
And the wrangling,

SPEAKER 3

How the danger sinks and swells,
By the sinking or the swelling in the anger of the
     bells—
Of the bells,—

BELLS

Of the bells, bells, bells, bells,
Bells, bells, bells—

SPEAKER 3

In the clamor and the clangor of the bells!

SPEAKER 4

Hear the tolling of the bells—

BELLS

Iron bells!

SPEAKER 4

What a world of solemn thought their monody[8]
    compels!
In the silence of the night,
How we shiver with affright
At the melancholy menace of their tone!
For every sound that floats
From the rust within their throats
Is a

BELLS

groan.

SPEAKER 4

And the people—ah, the people—
They that dwell up in the steeple,
All alone,
And who tolling, tolling, tolling,
In that muffled monotone,
Feel a glory in so rolling
On the human heart a stone—
They are neither man nor woman—
They are neither brute nor human—
They are Ghouls:—
And their king it is who tolls:—
And he

BELLS

rolls, rolls, rolls,

SPEAKER 4

Rolls
A paean[9] from the bells!
And his merry bosom swells
With the paean of the bells!
And he dances and he yells;

Keeping time, time, time
In a sort of Runic rhyme,
To the paean of the bells—
Of the bells:—

BELLS

Keeping time, time, time,
In a sort of Runic rhyme,
To the throbbing of the bells—

SPEAKER 4

Of the bells, bells, bells—

BELLS

To the sobbing of the bells;

SPEAKER 4

Keeping time, time, time,
As he knells,[10] knells, knells,
In a happy Runic rhyme,

BELLS

To the rolling of the bells—
Of the bells, bells, bells:—
To the tolling of the bells—
Of the bells, bells, bells, bells,
Bells, bells, bells—
To the moaning and the groaning of the bells.

[1] **Runic rhyme:** Norse chant

[2] **tintinnabulation:** jingling of bells

[3] **euphony:** pleasing or sweet sound

[4] **voluminously:** with great volume; loudly

[5] **turbulency:** wild commotion

[6] **expostulation:** protest

[7] **palpitating:** beating strongly, throbbing

[8] **monody:** song for the dead

[9] **paean:** song of triumph

[10] **knells:** rings mournfully

Most people, if asked to name an Australian song, would answer immediately, "Waltzing Matilda." But "Waltzing Matilda" was a poem before it was a song. It was written by A. B. (Banjo) Paterson sometime around 1895; the tune was added later. If the members of the Chorus know the tune, they might enjoy singing their lines. (They should be careful to sing all the choruses in the same key, however. A piano, guitar, or other instrument may be needed to get them started on the right pitch each time.)

WALTZING MATILDA

A. B. PATERSON

SPEAKERS

NARRATOR	THREE TROOPERS
SWAGMAN	SWAGMAN'S GHOST
CHORUS	

NARRATOR

Once a jolly swagman[1] camped by a billabong[2]
Under the shade of a coolabah[3] tree,
And he sang as he watched and waited till his billy[4]
    boiled,

SWAGMAN

You'll come a-waltzing, Matilda,[5] with me!

CHORUS

Waltzing[6] Matilda, waltzing Matilda,
You'll come a-waltzing, Matilda, with me!
And he sang as he watched and waited till his billy
    boiled,
You'll come a-waltzing Matilda, with me!

NARRATOR

Down come a jumbuck[7] to drink at the billabong,

Up jumped the swagman and grabbed him with glee,
And he sang as he stowed that jumbuck in his tucker-
bag,[8]

SWAGMAN

You'll come a-waltzing, Matilda, with me!

CHORUS

Waltzing Matilda, waltzing Matilda,
You'll come a-waltzing, Matilda, with me!
And he sang as he stowed that jumbuck in his tucker-
bag,
You'll come a-waltzing, Matilda, with me!

NARRATOR

Up rode the squatter[9] mounted on his thoroughbred,
Up rode the troopers, one, two, three.

THREE TROOPERS

Where's that jolly jumbuck you've got in your tucker-
bag?
You'll come a-waltzing, Matilda, with me!

CHORUS

Waltzing Matilda, waltzing Matilda,
You'll come a-waltzing, Matilda, with me!
Where's that jolly jumbuck you've got in your tucker-
bag?
You'll come a-waltzing, Matilda, with me!

NARRATOR

Up jumped the swagman and sprang into the billabong.

SWAGMAN

You'll never take me alive!

NARRATOR

said he.
And his ghost may be heard as you pass by that
    billabong:

SWAGMAN'S GHOST

You'll come a-waltzing, Matilda, with me!

CHORUS

Waltzing Matilda, waltzing Matilda,
You'll come a-waltzing, Matilda, with me!
And his ghost may be heard as you pass by that
    billabong,
You'll come a-waltzing, Matilda, with me!

---

[1] **swagman:** A swag is a bundle, usually consisting of blankets, clothing, cooking and eating utensils, and personal effects. A swagman is a man who carries a swag while traveling around on foot, usually in search of work.

[2] **billabong:** a creek or river (billa) that is dead (bong), or no longer flowing

[3] **coolabah:** a gum tree of the eucalyptus family that grows along riverbanks

[4] **billy:** a cooking pot; a pan for boiling water. The word is derived from *billa,* meaning water (by extension from creek or river).

[5] **matilda:** a slang term for a swag

[6] **waltzing:** probably from the German verb *walzen,* to walk or roam. Before this poem became well known, the expression "walking matilda" was more frequently used than "waltzing matilda."

[7] **jumbuck:** sheep

[8] **tucker-bag:** a bag for holding food (tucker)

[9] **squatter:** one who settles on government land with the intention of claiming ownership

This poem, set somewhere in the South during the Civil War, is a dialogue between a young Northern army soldier and his commanding officer. It seems that the young soldier, Achilles Deatheridge, made a serious mistake while on sentry duty last night. We aren't told what the mistake was, but we can guess that it had something to do with a suspicious-looking man who was prowling around the camp and who failed to halt and identify himself when Achilles challenged him. At the end of the poem, we find out that Achilles arrested the man and that he then discovered that his prisoner was General Ulysses S. Grant. Before you perform this poem, you may want to make sure your listeners have the background information they need to understand what's going on. You might announce the title and author, and then say something like this: "The two characters in this poem are members of one of the Union armies commanded by General Ulysses S. Grant during the Civil War."

ACHILLES DEATHERIDGE

EDGAR LEE MASTERS

SPEAKERS

CAPTAIN   ACHILLES

CAPTAIN

Your name is Achilles Deatheridge?
How old are you, my boy?

ACHILLES

I'm sixteen past, and I went to the war
From Athens, Illinois.

CAPTAIN

Achilles Deatheridge, you have done
A deed of dreadful note.

ACHILLES

It comes of his wearing a battered hat,
And a rusty, wrinkled coat.

CAPTAIN

Why, didn't you know how plain he is?
And didn't you ever hear
That he goes through the lines by day or night
Like a sooty cannoneer?
You must have been half dead for sleep,
For the dawn was growing bright.

ACHILLES

Well, Captain, I had stood right there
Since six o'clock last night.
I cocked my gun at the swish of the grass,
And how am I at fault
When a dangerous looking man won't stop
When a sentry hollers halt?
I cried out halt, and he only smiled
And waved his hand like that.
Why, any Johnnie could wear the coat
And any fellow the hat.
I hollered halt again, and he stopped
And lighted a fresh cigar.
I never noticed his shoulder badge,
And I never noticed a star.

CAPTAIN

So you arrested him? Well, Achilles,
When you hear the swish of the grass,
If it's General Grant inspecting the lines,
Hereafter let him pass.

The Passamaquoddy Indians lived in what is now the state of Maine and the province of New Brunswick, Canada. Lines 7 and 8 of this song of the stars refer to the constellation Ursa Major, or Great Bear. (The seven brightest stars in Ursa Major are also known as the Big Dipper.) It is interesting that the ancient Hebrews, Greeks, Romans, and North Americans all saw the same image—a bear—in this constellation. According to one Native American legend, the three stars that hunt the bear are Chickadee (who carries a cooking pot), Robin, and Moose-bird. These three pursue Bear across the sky, from the time she emerges from her den in the spring until late fall. At last they catch up with her, and Robin shoots her with his arrow. The blood from her wound stains Robin's breast and makes the leaves of the trees turn red. The hunt is eternal (line 9) because, although Bear dies, her spirit returns to the den and enters another bear, who will awaken next spring to begin the story all over again. The "road for the soul" mentioned in line 6 is probably the Milky Way.

THE STARS

PASSAMAQUODDY INDIANS

SPEAKERS

CHORUS	SPEAKER 3
SPEAKER 1	SPEAKER 4
SPEAKER 2	

CHORUS

For we are the stars. For we sing.

SPEAKER 1

For we sing with our light.

SPEAKER 2

For we are birds made of fire.

SPEAKER 3

For we spread our wings over the sky.

SPEAKER 4

Our light is a voice.

CHORUS

We cut a road for the soul for its journey through death.

SPEAKER 2

For three of our number are hunters.

SPEAKER 4

For these three hunt a bear.

SPEAKER 1

For there never yet was a time when these three didn't
    hunt.

SPEAKER 3

For we face the hills with disdain.

CHORUS

This is the song of the stars.

In *Alice in Wonderland,* Alice complains to the caterpillar that her brain is so muddled by all the growing and shrinking she has been doing that she can't recite the poems she once knew by heart. Whenever she tries, the words come out all wrong. "Repeat 'You are old, Father William,'" demands the caterpillar. He is referring to a moralistic poem by Robert Southey that begins with these words. Entitled "The Old Man's Comforts and How He Gained Them," it consists of three questions asked by a young man and the three answers given by old Father William. The point of the poem is that sensible living and religious faith in youth lead to health and contentment in old age. Alice tries her best to recite Southey's poem, but what comes out is this parody, or fun-poking imitation.

FATHER WILLIAM

LEWIS CARROLL

SPEAKERS

YOUNG MAN	FATHER WILLIAM
NARRATOR	

YOUNG MAN

You are old, Father William,

NARRATOR

the young man said,

YOUNG MAN

And your hair has become very white;
And yet you incessantly stand on your head—
Do you think, at your age, it is right?

FATHER WILLIAM

In my youth,

NARRATOR

Father William replied to his son,

FATHER WILLIAM

I feared it might injure the brain;
But, now that I'm perfectly sure I have none,
Why, I do it again and again.

YOUNG MAN

You are old,

NARRATOR

said the youth,

YOUNG MAN

as I mentioned before,
And have grown most uncommonly fat;
Yet you turned a back-somersault in at the door—
Pray, what is the reason of that?

FATHER WILLIAM

In my youth,

NARRATOR

said the sage, as he shook his gray locks,

FATHER WILLIAM

I kept all my limbs very supple
By the use of this ointment—one shilling the box—
Allow me to sell you a couple?

YOUNG MAN

You are old,

NARRATOR

said the youth,

YOUNG MAN

and your jaws are too weak
For anything tougher than suet;

Yet you finished the goose, with the bones and the
     beak—
Pray how did you manage to do it?

FATHER WILLIAM

In my youth,

NARRATOR

said his father,

FATHER WILLIAM

I took to the law,
And argued each case with my wife;
And the muscular strength which it gave to my jaw,
Has lasted the rest of my life.

YOUNG MAN

You are old,

NARRATOR

said the youth,

YOUNG MAN

one would hardly suppose
That your eye was as steady as ever;
Yet you balanced an eel on the end of your nose—
What made you so awfully clever?

FATHER WILLIAM

I have answered three questions, and that is enough,

NARRATOR

Said his father;

FATHER WILLIAM

don't give yourself airs!
Do you think I can listen all day to such stuff?
Be off, or I'll kick you downstairs.

The poems that follow are taken from a book of poems entitled *Spoon River Anthology*. Spoon River, Illinois, is a fictional town created by the poet Edgar Lee Masters. In each poem, a deceased citizen of Spoon River speaks from the grave about the experiences and lessons of his or her life. The speakers address us, the audience, as if we were visitors to their graves in the cemetery on the hill. For example, Hannah Armstrong tells us about the time she went to Washington to ask a favor from a man who once boarded (took his meals) at her house—President Abraham Lincoln. Griffy the cooper (barrel-maker) scolds us for having an outlook on life that's as narrow as a tub. Mrs. George Reece gives us a helpful piece of advice. In this presentation, verses from "The Hill," the first poem in *Spoon River Anthology,* are read by two narrators. These verses help to set the scene. The narrators also call out the name of each speaker in turn, so the audience will know who is addressing them.

POEMS FROM *SPOON RIVER ANTHOLOGY*

EDGAR LEE MASTERS

SPEAKERS

NARRATOR 1	LUCINDA MATLOCK
NARRATOR 2	GEORGE GRAY
HANNAH ARMSTRONG	GRIFFY THE COOPER
COONEY POTTER	SETH COMPTON
FIDDLER JONES	MRS. GEORGE REECE

NARRATOR 1

Where are Elmer, Herman, Bert, Tom and Charley,
The weak of will, the strong of arm, the clown, the
   boozer, the fighter?

NARRATORS 1 AND 2

All, all, are sleeping on the hill.

NARRATOR 2

Where are Ella, Kate, Mag, Lizzie and Edith,

The tender heart, the simple soul, the loud, the proud,
   the happy one?—

All, all, are sleeping on the hill.

Hannah Armstrong

HANNAH ARMSTRONG

I wrote him a letter asking him for old times' sake
To discharge my sick boy from the army;
But maybe he couldn't read it.
Then I went to town and had James Garber,
Who wrote beautifully, write him a letter;
But maybe that was lost in the mails.
So I traveled all the way to Washington.
I was more than an hour finding the White House.
And when I found it they turned me away,
Hiding their smiles. Then I thought:
"Oh, well, he ain't the same as when I boarded him
And he and my husband worked together
And all of us called him Abe, there in Menard."
As a last attempt I turned to a guard and said:
"Please say it's old Aunt Hannah Armstrong
From Illinois, come to see him about her sick boy
In the army."
Well, just in a moment they let me in!
And when he saw me he broke in a laugh,
And dropped his business as president,
And wrote in his own hand Doug's discharge,
Talking the while of the early days,
And telling stories.

Cooney Potter

COONEY POTTER

I inherited forty acres from my Father
And, by working my wife, my two sons and two
    daughters
From dawn to dusk, I acquired
A thousand acres. But not content,
Wishing to own two thousand acres,
I bustled through the years with axe and plow,
Toiling, denying myself, my wife, my sons, my
    daughters.
Squire Higbee wrongs me to say
That I died from smoking Red Eagle cigars.
Eating hot pie and gulping coffee
During the scorching hours of harvest time
Brought me here ere I had reached my sixtieth year.

NARRATOR 1

Fiddler Jones

FIDDLER JONES

The earth keeps some vibration going
There in your heart, and that is you.
And if the people find you can fiddle,
Why, fiddle you must, for all your life.
What do you see, a harvest of clover?
Or a meadow to walk through to the river?
The wind's in the corn; you rub your hands
For beeves[1] hereafter ready for market;
Or else you hear the rustle of skirts
Like the girls when dancing at Little Grove.
To Cooney Potter a pillar of dust
Or whirling leaves meant ruinous drouth;
They looked to me like Red-Head Sammy
Stepping it off, to "Toor-a-Loor."
How could I till[2] my forty acres,

Not to speak of getting more,
With a medley of horns, bassoons and piccolos
Stirred in my brain by crows and robins
And the creak of a wind-mill—only these?
And I never started to plow in my life
That someone did not stop in the road
And take me away to a dance or picnic.
I ended up with forty acres;
I ended up with a broken fiddle—
And a broken laugh, and a thousand memories,
And not a single regret.

NARRATOR 2
Lucinda Matlock

LUCINDA MATLOCK
I went to the dances at Chandlerville,
And played snap-out at Winchester.
One time we changed partners,
Driving home in the moonlight of middle June,
And then I found Davis.
We were married and lived together for seventy years,
Enjoying, working, raising the twelve children,
Eight of whom we lost
Ere I had reached the age of sixty.
I spun, I wove, I kept the house, I nursed the sick,
I made the garden, and for holiday
Rambled over the fields where sang the larks,
And by Spoon River gathering many a shell,
And many a flower and medicinal weed—
Shouting to the wooded hills, singing to the green
        valleys.
At ninety-six I had lived enough, that is all,
And passed to a sweet repose.
What is this I hear of sorrow and weariness,
Anger, discontent and drooping hopes?

Degenerate[3] sons and daughters,
Life is too strong for you—
It takes life to love Life.

George Gray

GEORGE GRAY

I have studied many times
The marble which was chiseled for me—
A boat with a furled sail at rest in a harbor.
In truth it pictures not my destination
But my life.
For love was offered me and I shrank from its
        disillusionment;
Sorrow knocked at my door, but I was afraid;
Ambition called to me, but I dreaded the chances.
Yet all the while I hungered for meaning in my life.
And now I know that we must lift the sail
And catch the winds of destiny
Wherever they drive the boat.
To put meaning in one's life may end in madness,
But life without meaning is the torture
Of restlessness and vague desire—
It is a boat longing for the sea and yet afraid.

NARRATOR 2

Griffy the Cooper

GRIFFY

The cooper should know about tubs.
But I learned about life as well,
And you who loiter around these graves
Think you know life.
You think your eye sweeps about a wide horizon,
        perhaps.

In truth you are only looking around the interior of
    your tub.
You cannot lift yourself to its rim
And see the outer world of things,
And at the same time see yourself.
You are submerged in the tub of yourself—
Taboos and rules and appearances
Are the staves of your tub.
Break them and dispel the witchcraft
Of thinking your tub is life!
And that you know life!

NARRATOR 1

Seth Compton

SETH COMPTON

When I died, the circulating library[4]
Which I built up for Spoon River,
And managed for the good of inquiring minds,
Was sold at auction on the public square,
As if to destroy the last vestige
Of my memory and influence.
For those of you who could not see the virtue
Of knowing Volney's "Ruins"[5] as well as Butler's
    "Analogy"[6]
And "Faust"[7] as well as "Evangeline,"[8]
Were really the power in the village,
And often you asked me,
"What is the use of knowing the evil in the world?"
I am out of your way now, Spoon River,
Choose your own good and call it good.
For I could never make you see
That no one knows what is good
Who knows not what is evil;
And no one knows what is true
Who knows not what is false.

Mrs. George Reece

MRS. GEORGE REECE

To this generation I would say:
Memorize some bit of verse of truth or beauty.
It may serve a turn in your life.
My husband had nothing to do
With the fall of the bank—he was only a cashier.
The wreck was due to the president, Thomas Rhodes,
And his vain, unscrupulous son.
Yet my husband was sent to prison,
And I was left with the children,
To feed and clothe and school them.
And I did it, and sent them forth
Into the world all clean and strong,
And all through the wisdom of Pope, the poet:
"Act well your part, there all the honor lies."

NARRATORS 1 AND 2

Where are Uncle Isaac and Aunt Emily,
And old Towny Kincaid and Sevigne Houghton,
And Major Walker who had talked
With venerable men of the revolution?—
All, all, are sleeping on the hill.

[1] **beeves:** beefs; that is, cattle   [2] **till:** cultivate

[3] **degenerate:** inferior to those who came before

[4] **circulating library:** a library whose books may be borrowed by the public

[5] **Volney's** *Ruins:* a book on the philosophy of history by a Frenchman

[6] **Butler's** *Analogy:* religious writings by an English bishop

[7] *Faust:* a dramatic poem by the German poet Goethe, about a man who
  sells his soul to the Devil in return for knowledge, power, and worldly
  pleasures

[8] *Evangeline:* a narrative poem by Longfellow, about a group of French
  settlers who, in 1755, were deported from what is now eastern Canada to
  Louisiana

This amusing poem by Carl Sandburg is arranged for three speakers, each of whom speaks three times; but it could also be read by . . . how many speakers? (That's just an easy little warm-up problem, to get you in the mood.) It might be fun to have one or more non-speaking performers sit at a table at the front of the room and pretend to work arithmetic problems while the speakers read their lines. The problem-workers could show all the signs of suffering and struggle that people usually show when they try to do arithmetic.

ARITHMETIC

CARL SANDBURG

SPEAKERS

SPEAKER 1   SPEAKER 3
SPEAKER 2

SPEAKER 1

Arithmetic is where numbers fly like pigeons in and out
of your head.

SPEAKER 2

Arithmetic tells you how many you lose or win if you
know how many you had before you lost or won.

SPEAKER 3

Arithmetic is seven eleven all good children go to
heaven—or five six bundle of sticks.

SPEAKER 1

Arithmetic is numbers you squeeze from your head to
your hand to your pencil to your paper till you get
the answer.

SPEAKER 3

Arithmetic is where the answer is right and everything

is nice and you can look out of the window and see the blue sky—or the answer is wrong and you have to start all over and try again and see how it comes out this time.

SPEAKER 2

If you take a number and double it and double it again and then double it a few more times, the number gets bigger and bigger and goes higher and higher and only arithmetic can tell you what the number is when you decide to quit doubling.

SPEAKER 3

Arithmetic is where you have to multiply—and you carry the multiplication table in your head and hope you won't lose it.

SPEAKER 1

If you have two animal crackers, one good and one bad, and you eat one and a striped zebra with streaks all over him eats the other, how many animal crackers will you have if somebody offers you five six seven and you say No no no and you say Nay nay nay and you say Nix nix nix?

SPEAKER 2

If you ask your mother for one fried egg for breakfast and she gives you two fried eggs and you eat both of them, who is better in arithmetic, you or your mother?

To the Pygmies of Gabon, Africa, the thousands of different forms that appear in nature are all manifestations (showings) of a universal life force that exists everywhere. This life force expresses itself in movement and sound. The four animals mentioned in the poem below live in four different environments: water (fish), air (bird), earth (marmot—a rodent belonging to the same family as the woodchuck), and trees (monkey).

ALL LIVES, ALL DANCES, AND ALL IS LOUD

PYGMIES OF GABON, AFRICA

SPEAKERS

SPEAKER 1	SPEAKER 3
SPEAKER 2	SPEAKER 4

SPEAKER 1

The fish does . . . HIP
The bird does . . . VISS
The marmot does . . . GNAN

SPEAKER 2

I throw myself to the left,
I turn myself to the right,
I act the fish,
Which darts in the water, which darts
Which twists about, which leaps—

ALL SPEAKERS

All lives, all dances, and all is loud.

SPEAKER 1

The fish does . . . HIP
The bird does . . . VISS
The marmot does . . . GNAN

SPEAKER 3

The bird flies away,
It flies, flies, flies,
Goes, returns, passes,
Climbs, soars and drops.
I act the bird—

ALL SPEAKERS

All lives, all dances, and all is loud.

SPEAKER 1

The fish does . . . HIP
The bird does . . . VISS
The marmot does . . . GNAN

SPEAKER 4

The monkey from branch to branch,
Runs, bounds, and leaps,
With his wife, with his brat,
His mouth full, his tail in the air,
There goes the monkey! There goes the monkey!

ALL SPEAKERS

All lives, all dances, and all is loud.

"I Gave My Love a Cherry" is what experts on folklore call a courtship riddle song. The verses of such a song are arranged in sets of three. In the first verse below, a suitor brags about the gifts he has given his sweetheart, all of which sound impossible. In the second verse, his listeners challenge him to explain how such things can exist. In the third verse, the suitor gives the answers to the riddles.

I GAVE MY LOVE A CHERRY

ANONYMOUS

SPEAKERS

SPEAKER 1   SPEAKER 3
SPEAKER 2   SPEAKER 4

SPEAKER 1

I gave my love a cherry without a stone,
I gave my love a chicken without a bone,
I gave my love a ring that has no end,
I gave my love a baby that has no cryin'.

SPEAKER 2

How can there be a cherry that has no stone?

SPEAKER 3

How can there be a chicken that has no bone?

SPEAKER 4

How can there be a ring that has no end?

SPEAKER 2

How can there be a baby that has no cryin'?

SPEAKER 1

A cherry when it's bloomin', it has no stone;
A chicken when it's in the egg, it has no bone;

A ring when it's rollin', it has no end;
A baby when it's sleepin', it has no cryin'.

SPEAKER 2

I gave my love an apple without a core,
I gave my love a dwelling without a door,
I gave my love a palace wherein she [he] might be,
That she [he] might unlock it without a key.

SPEAKER 1

How can there be an apple without a core?

SPEAKER 3

How can there be a dwelling without a door?

SPEAKER 4

How can there be a palace wherein she [he] might be,
That she [he] might unlock it without a key?

SPEAKER 2

My head it is an apple without a core.
My mind it is a dwelling without a door.
My heart it is a palace wherein she [he] might be,
That she [he] might unlock it without a key.

THE FLATTERED FLYING FISH

E. V. RIEU

SPEAKERS

NARRATOR   FLYING FISH
SHARK

NARRATOR

Said the Shark to the Flying Fish over the phone:

SHARK

(speaking into the phone)
Will you join me tonight? I am dining alone.
Let me order a nice little dinner for two!
And come as you are, in your shimmering blue.

NARRATOR

Said the Flying Fish:

FLYING FISH

(into the phone)
Fancy remembering me,
And the dress that I wore at the Porpoises' tea!

SHARK

How could I forget?

NARRATOR

said the Shark in his guile:

SHARK

I expect you at eight!

NARRATOR

and rang off with a smile.

(The shark hangs up the phone.)

NARRATOR

She has powdered her nose; she has put on her things;
She is off with one flap of her luminous wings.
(sadly)

O little one, lovely, lighthearted and vain,
The Moon will not shine on your beauty again!

Since this poem is so short, you might like to follow it immediately with "Take Time" (on the next page), to make a longer performance. With the help of two more people, the two speakers who read "Sea-Sand and Sorrow" can also read "Take Time." All four speakers should be "onstage" for both poems.

SEA-SAND AND SORROW

CHRISTINA ROSSETTI

SPEAKERS

SPEAKER 1   SPEAKER 2

SPEAKER 1

What are heavy?

SPEAKER 2

Sea-sand and sorrow.
What are brief?

SPEAKER 1

To-day and to-morrow.
What are frail?

SPEAKER 2

Spring blossoms and youth.
What are deep?

SPEAKER 1

The ocean . . .

SPEAKERS 1 AND 2

and truth.

TAKE TIME

ANONYMOUS

SPEAKERS

SPEAKER 1   SPEAKER 3
SPEAKER 2   SPEAKER 4

SPEAKER 1

Take time to work —
It is the price of success.
Take time to think —
It is the source of power.

SPEAKER 2

Take time to play —
It is the secret of perpetual youth.
Take time to read —
It is the fountain of wisdom.

SPEAKER 3

Take time to be friendly —
It is the road to happiness.
Take time to dream —
It is hitching your wagon to a star.

SPEAKER 4

Take time to love and to be loved —
It is the privilege of the gods.
Take time to look around —
It is too short a day to be selfish.

ALL SPEAKERS

Take time to laugh —
It is the music of the soul.

On January 22, 1878, a newspaper in London, England, reported that the Akond of Swat was dead. "Who or what," you may ask, "was the Akond of Swat?" The same question occurred to Edward Lear, a well-known writer of light verse, and he expanded it into the twenty questions that make up this amusing poem. The humor of the poem lies mostly in the cleverness with which Lear works in words that rhyme with "Swat." After each "Swat" rhyme, the listener thinks, "That must be the last one. Lear can't possibly come up with another." But Lear does come up with another, and another, and yet another, until he reaches a total of nineteen. In this presentation, Speaker 4 has the fun of pronouncing the "Swat" rhymes. He or she should say them loudly and clearly, with emphasis on the "ah" sound of the vowel. Note that the word "what" must be mispronounced slightly to make it rhyme with "Swat." (By the way, the Akond was the ruler of the state of Swat in northern India. Since 1947, when India was partitioned, Swat has been part of Pakistan.)

THE AKOND OF SWAT

EDWARD LEAR

SPEAKERS

SPEAKER 1   SPEAKER 4
SPEAKER 2   CHORUS
SPEAKER 3

SPEAKER 1
  Who,

SPEAKER 2
  or why,

SPEAKER 3
  or which,

SPEAKER 4
  or what

CHORUS

Is the Akond of Swat?

SPEAKER 1

Is he tall or short,

SPEAKER 2

or dark, or fair?

SPEAKER 3

Does he sit on a stool or a sofa or chair,

SPEAKER 4

or SQUAT,

CHORUS

The Akond of Swat?

SPEAKER 1

Is he wise or foolish,

SPEAKER 2

young or old?

SPEAKER 3

Does he drink his soup and his coffee cold,

SPEAKER 4

or HOT,

CHORUS

The Akond of Swat?

SPEAKER 2

Does he sing or whistle,

SPEAKER 3

jabber or talk?

SPEAKER 1

When riding abroad, does he gallop or walk,

SPEAKER 4

or TROT,

CHORUS

The Akond of Swat?

SPEAKER 3

Does he wear a turban, a fez, or a hat?

SPEAKER 2

Does he sleep on a mattress, a bed,

SPEAKER 1

or a mat,

SPEAKER 4

or a COT,

CHORUS

The Akond of Swat?

SPEAKER 1

When he writes a copy in round-hand size,

SPEAKER 3

Does he cross his t's

SPEAKER 2

and finish his i's

SPEAKER 4

with a DOT,

CHORUS

The Akond of Swat?

SPEAKER 1

Can he write a letter concisely clear,
Without a speck or a smudge or smear

SPEAKER 4

or BLOT,

CHORUS

The Akond of Swat?

SPEAKER 2

Do his people like him extremely well?
Or do they, whenever they can, rebel,

SPEAKER 4

or PLOT,

CHORUS

At the Akond of Swat?

SPEAKER 3

If he catches them then, either old or young,
Does he have them chopped in pieces or hung,

SPEAKER 4

or SHOT,

CHORUS

The Akond of Swat?

SPEAKER 2

Does he study the wants of his own dominion?
Or doesn't he care for public opinion

SPEAKER 4

a JOT,

CHORUS

The Akond of Swat?

SPEAKER 1

To amuse his mind do his people show him
Pictures,

SPEAKER 3

or anyone's last new poem,

SPEAKER 4

or WHAT,

CHORUS

The Akond of Swat?

SPEAKER 2

At night if he suddenly screams and wakes,
Do they bring him only a few small cakes,

SPEAKER 4

or a LOT,

CHORUS

The Akond of Swat?

SPEAKER 1

Does he live on turnips, tea, or tripe?

SPEAKER 3

Does he like his shawl to be marked with a stripe,

SPEAKER 4

or a DOT,

CHORUS

The Akond of Swat?

SPEAKER 2

Is he quiet, or always making a fuss?

SPEAKER 3

Is his steward a Swiss,

SPEAKER 2

or a Swede,

SPEAKER 1

or a Russ,

SPEAKER 4

or a SCOT,

CHORUS

The Akond of Swat?

SPEAKER 3

Does he like to sit by the calm blue wave?

SPEAKER 2

Or to sleep and snore in a dark green cave,

SPEAKER 4

or a GROT,

CHORUS

The Akond of Swat?

SPEAKER 1

Does he drink small beer from a silver jug?

SPEAKER 2

Or a bowl?

SPEAKER 3

or a glass?

SPEAKER 2

or a cup?

SPEAKER 1

or a mug?

SPEAKER 4

or a POT?

CHORUS

The Akond of Swat?

SPEAKER 3

Does he beat his wife with a gold-topped pipe,
When she lets the gooseberries grow too ripe,

SPEAKER 4

or ROT,

CHORUS

The Akond of Swat?

SPEAKER 1

Does he wear a white tie when he dines with friends,
And tie it neat in a bow with ends,

SPEAKER 4

or a KNOT,

CHORUS

The Akond of Swat?

SPEAKER 2

Does he like new cream, and hate mince-pies?

SPEAKER 3

When he looks at the sun does he wink his eyes,

SPEAKER 4

or NOT,

CHORUS

The Akond of Swat?

SPEAKER 1

Does he teach his subjects to roast and bake?

SPEAKER 2

Does he sail about on an inland lake

SPEAKER 4

in a YACHT,

CHORUS

The Akond of Swat?

SPEAKER 1

Someone, or nobody, knows I wot
Who,

SPEAKER 2

or which,

SPEAKER 3

or why,

SPEAKER 4

or *what*

CHORUS

Is the Akond of Swat!

The poem that follows is a slightly shortened version of Tennyson's *Morte d'Arthur* ("The Death of Arthur"). The story it tells is just one of a large group of related stories that make up the Arthurian legend. Some of these stories tell about Arthur's life: about how Merlin the Magician educated him by turning him into various animals; about how he proved his right to be king by pulling a sword out of a stone; about how he obtained the magical sword Excalibur from the ruler of an enchanted lake; and about how he courted and won Guinevere but later lost her to his best friend, Sir Lancelot. Other stories relate the adventures of the knights who fought for King Arthur and had places of honor at his Round Table.

Tennyson's poem opens with the line "So all day long the noise of battle roll'd . . . ." It is Arthur's last battle, and it is a particularly bitter one for him because he is fighting against his nephew, Mordred, who has turned traitor. By nightfall, all but one of Arthur's knights have been killed, and the king himself has been badly wounded by a blow from Mordred's sword that cut through his helmet and into his skull.

THE DEATH OF KING ARTHUR

ALFRED, LORD TENNYSON

SPEAKERS

NARRATOR 1   SIR BEDIVERE
NARRATOR 2   KING ARTHUR
NARRATOR 3

NARRATOR 1

So all day long the noise of battle roll'd
Among the mountains by the winter sea,
Until King Arthur's table, man by man,
Had fallen in Lyonnesse about their lord,
King Arthur.

NARRATOR 2

Then, because his wound was deep,
The bold Sir Bedivere uplifted him,
Sir Bedivere, the last of all his knights,
And bore him to a chapel nigh the field,
A broken chancel[1] with a broken cross,
That stood on a dark straight of barren land.

NARRATOR 1

On one side lay the ocean, and on one
Lay a great water, and the moon was full.
Then spake King Arthur to Sir Bedivere:

KING ARTHUR

I am so deeply smitten thro' the helm[2]
That without help I cannot last till morn.
Thou therefore take my brand[3] Excalibur,
Which was my pride; for thou rememberest how
In those old days, one summer noon, an arm
Rose up from out the bosom of the lake,

Clothed in white samite,[4] mystic, wonderful,
Holding the sword—and how I row'd across
And took it, and have worn it, like a king;
And, wheresoever I am sung or told
In aftertime, this also shall be known.
But now delay not; take Excalibur,
And fling him far into the middle mere;[5]
Watch what thou seest, and lightly bring me word.

NARRATOR 2

To him replied the bold Sir Bedivere:

SIR BEDIVERE

It is not meet,[6] Sir King, to leave thee thus,
Aidless, alone, and smitten thro' the helm.
A little thing may harm a wounded man.
Yet I thy hest[7] will all perform at full,
Watch what I see, and lightly bring thee word.

NARRATOR 2

So saying, from the ruin'd shrine he stept
And in the moon athwart[8] the place of tombs,
Where lay the mighty bones of ancient men,
Old knights, and over them the sea-wind sang
Shrill, chill, with flakes of foam. He, stepping down
By zigzag paths and juts of pointed rock,
Came on the shining levels of the lake.

NARRATOR 1

There drew he forth the brand Excalibur,
And o'er him, drawing it, the winter moon,
Brightening the skirts of a long cloud, ran forth
And sparkled keen with frost against the hilt;[9]
For all the haft[9] twinkled with diamond sparks,
Myriads of topaz-lights, and jacinth-work[10]
Of subtlest jewelry.

NARRATOR 2

He gazed so long
That both his eyes were dazzled, as he stood
This way and that dividing the swift mind,
In act to throw; but at the last it seem'd
Better to leave Excalibur conceal'd
There in the many-knotted water-flags,
That whistled stiff and dry about the marge.[11]
So strode he back slow to the wounded king.

NARRATOR 1

Then spake King Arthur to Sir Bedivere:

KING ARTHUR

Hast thou perform'd my mission which I gave?
What is it thou hast seen, or what hast heard?

NARRATOR 2

And answer made the bold Sir Bedivere:

SIR BEDIVERE

I heard the ripple washing in the reeds,
And the wild water lapping on the crag.

NARRATOR 1

To whom replied King Arthur, faint and pale:

KING ARTHUR

Thou hast betray'd thy nature and thy name,
Not rendering true answer, as beseem'd[12]
Thy fealty,[13] nor like a noble knight;
For surer sign had[14] follow'd, either hand,
Or voice, or else a motion of the mere.
This is a shameful thing for men to lie.
Yet now, I charge thee, quickly go again
As thou art lief[15] and dear, and do the thing
I bade thee, watch, and lightly bring me word.

NARRATOR 2

Then went Sir Bedivere the second time
Across the ridge, and paced beside the mere,
Counting the dewey pebbles, fix'd in thought;
But when he saw the wonder of the hilt,
How curiously and strangely chased,[16] he smote
His palms together, and he cried aloud:

SIR BEDIVERE

And if indeed I cast the brand away,
Surely a precious thing, one worthy note,
Should thus be lost forever from the earth,
Which might have pleased the eyes of many men.
What good should follow this, if this were done?
What harm, undone? deep harm to disobey,
Seeing obedience is the bond of rule.
Were it well to obey then, if a king demand
An act unprofitable, against himself?
The king is sick, and knows not what he does.

NARRATOR 2

So spake he, clouded with his own conceit,
And hid Excalibur the second time,
And so strode back slow to the wounded king.

NARRATOR 1

Then spoke King Arthur, breathing heavily:

KING ARTHUR

What is it thou hast seen, or what hast heard?

NARRATOR 2

And answer made the bold Sir Bedivere:

SIR BEDIVERE

I heard the water lapping on the crag,
And the long ripple washing in the reeds.

NARRATOR 1

To whom replied King Arthur, much in wrath:

KING ARTHUR

Ah, miserable and unkind, untrue,
Unknightly, traitor-hearted! Woe is me!
For thou, the latest-left of all my knights,
In whom should meet the offices of all,
Thou wouldst betray me for the precious hilt
Either from lust of gold, or like a girl
Valuing the giddy pleasure of the eyes.
Yet, for a man may fail in duty twice,
And the third time may prosper, get thee hence;
But, if thou spare[17] to fling Excalibur,
I will arise and slay thee with my hands.

NARRATOR 2

Then quickly rose Sir Bedivere, and ran,
And, leaping down the ridges lightly, plunged
Among the bulrush-beds, and clutch'd the sword,
And strongly wheel'd and threw it. The great brand
Made lightnings in the splendor of the moon,
And flashing round and round, and whirl'd in an arch,
Shot like a streamer of the northern morn, . . .
So flash'd and fell the brand Excalibur.

NARRATOR 3

But ere he dipt the surface, rose an arm
Clothed in white samite, mystic, wonderful,
And caught him by the hilt, and brandish'd[18] him
Three times, and drew him under in the mere.

NARRATOR 2

And lightly went the other to the King.

NARRATOR 1

Then spoke King Arthur, drawing thicker breath:

KING ARTHUR

Now see I by thine eyes that this is done.
Speak out: what is it thou hast heard or seen?

NARRATOR 2

And answer made the bold Sir Bedivere:

SIR BEDIVERE

Sir King, I closed mine eyelids, lest the gems
Should blind my purpose, for I never saw
Nor shall see, here or elsewhere, till I die,
Not tho' I live three lives of mortal men,
So great a miracle as yonder hilt.
Then with both hands I flung him, wheeling him;
But when I look'd again, behold an arm,
Clothed in white samite, mystic, wonderful,
That caught him by the hilt, and brandish'd him
Three times, and drew him under in the mere.

NARRATOR 1

And answer made King Arthur, breathing hard:

KING ARTHUR

My end draws nigh; 'tis time that I were gone.
Make broad thy shoulders to receive my weight,
And bear me to the margin; yet I fear
My wound hath taken cold, and I shall die.

NARRATOR 1

So saying, from the pavement he half rose,
Slowly, with pain, reclining on his arm,
And looking wistfully with wide blue eyes
As in a picture.

NARRATOR 2

Him Sir Bedivere
Remorsefully regarded thro' his tears,

And would have spoken, but he found not words,
Then took with care, and kneeling on one knee,
O'er both his shoulders drew the languid hands,
And rising bore him thro' the place of tombs.

NARRATOR 1

But, as he walk'd, King Arthur panted hard,
Like one that feels a nightmare on his bed
When all the house is mute. So sigh'd the King,
Muttering and murmuring at his ear,

KING ARTHUR

Quick, quick!
I fear it is too late, and I shall die.

NARRATOR 2

But the other swiftly strode from ridge to ridge,
Clothed with his breath, and looking, as he walk'd
Larger than human on the frozen hills.

NARRATOR 1

And on a sudden, lo! the level lake,
And the long glories of the winter moon.

NARRATOR 3

Then saw they how there hove[19] a dusky barge,
Dark as a funeral scarf from stem to stern,
Beneath them; and descending they were ware[20]
That all the decks were dense with stately forms
Black-stoled, black-hooded, like a dream—by these
Three Queens with crowns of gold—and from them
　　rose
A cry that shiver'd to the tingling stars,
And, as it were one voice, an agony
Of lamentation, like a wind, that shrills
All night in a waste land, where no one comes,
Or hath come, since the making of the world.

NARRATOR 1

Then murmur'd Arthur,

KING ARTHUR

Place me in the barge.

NARRATOR 3

And to the barge they came. There those three Queens
Put forth their hands, and took the King, and wept.
But she that rose the tallest of them all
And fairest, laid his head upon her lap,
And loosed the shatter'd casque,²¹ and chafed his
    hands,
And call'd him by his name, complaining loud,
And dropping bitter tears against his brow
Striped with dark blood: for all his face was white
And colorless, and like the wither'd moon
Smote by the fresh beam of the springing east.

NARRATOR 1

So like a shatter'd column lay the King,
Not like that Arthur who, with lance in rest,
From spur to plume a star of tournament,
Shot thro the lists²² at Camelot, and charged
Before the eyes of ladies and of kings.

NARRATOR 2

Then loudly cried the bold Sir Bedivere,

SIR BEDIVERE

Ah! my Lord Arthur, whither shall I go?
Where shall I hide my forehead and my eyes?
For now I see the true old times are dead,
When every morning brought a noble chance,
And every chance brought out a noble knight.
But now the whole ROUND TABLE is dissolved
Which was an image of the mighty world;

And I, the last, go forth companionless,
And the days darken round me, and the years,
Among new men, strange faces, other minds.

NARRATOR 1

And slowly answer'd Arthur from the barge:

KING ARTHUR

The old order changeth, yielding place to new,
And God fulfills himself in many ways,
Lest one good custom should corrupt the world.
Comfort thyself: what comfort is in me?
I have lived my life, and that which I have done
May He within himself make pure! but thou,
If thou shouldst never see my face again,
Pray for my soul. More things are wrought by prayer
Than this world dreams of. Wherefore, let thy voice
Rise like a fountain for me night and day. . . .
But now farewell. I am going a long way
With these thou seest—if indeed I go—
For all my mind is clouded with a doubt—
To the island-valley of Avilion;
Where falls not hail, or rain, or any snow
Nor ever wind blows loudly, but it lies
Deep-meadow'd, happy, fair with orchard lawns
And bowery hollows crown'd with summer sea,
Where I will heal me of my grievous wound.

NARRATOR 1

So said he, and the barge with oar and sail
Moved from the brink, like some full-breasted swan
That, fluting a wild carol ere her death,
Ruffles her pure cold plume, and takes the flood
With swarthy webs.

NARRATOR 2

Long stood Sir Bedivere

Revolving many memories, till the hull
Look'd one black dot against the verge of dawn,
And on the mere the wailing died away.

This Chinese poem dates back to the first century B.C. In those days it was the custom for two people who wished to formalize their friendship to hold a little ceremony in which they promised to be loyal and true to each other. They would set up an altar of earth and recite this oath. The phrase "SHANG YA," in the first line of the oath, is a name for the Deity in Mandarin Chinese. In this context, it probably means something like "Before God I declare . . . ."

OATH OF FRIENDSHIP

ARTHUR WALEY, TRANSLATOR

SPEAKERS

SPEAKER 1   SPEAKER 2

SPEAKERS 1 AND 2

SHANG YA!
I want to be your friend
For ever and ever without break or decay.
When the hills are all flat
And the rivers are all dry,
When it lightens and thunders in winter,
When it rains and snows in summer,
When Heaven and Earth mingle—
Not till then will I part from you.

Our word for a long, roundabout, adventurous journey comes from the name of the most famous wanderer in Western literature: Odysseus. Odysseus was the king of the Greek island of Ithaka, and his odyssey took him to twelve dangerous places over a period of ten years. He was trying to get home to Ithaka from Troy, a city in Asia Minor, where he had helped the Greeks win victory in a ten-year war. Why did it take Odysseus so long to reach his homeland? You will learn the answer to that question when you read the terrible curse that is called down on his head in "Odysseus and the Kyklops."

At the beginning of this episode, we find Odysseus at the court of Alkinoos, king of the Phaiakians. This is Odysseus' last stop before home. He is alone, having lost all his companions in one or another of his earlier adventures. Although Odysseus avoids identifying himself, Alkinoos realizes he is a man of some importance and entertains him lavishly with feasts and athletic contests. Finally, noticing that Odysseus weeps when he hears the king's minstrel sing songs of the Trojan War, Alkinoos insists that his guest tell his name and his story.

GLOSSARY OF NAMES

Odysseus /ō dĭs' ē əs/ The king of Ithaka and one of the leaders of the Greeks in the Trojan War, known for his ingenuity and cunning as well as for his courage

Kyklops /kī' klŏps/ One of a savage race of one-eyed giants

Kyklopes /kī klō' pēz/ Plural of *Kyklops*

Polyphemos /pŏl ə fē' məs/ The Kyklops whose cave the Greeks unwisely enter

Alkinoos /ăl kī' nō əs/ The king to whose shores Odysseus swims after his ship is wrecked

Laertes /lā ār' tēz/ The father of Odysseus, now an old man

Ithaka /ĭth' ə kə/ A Greek island in the Ionian Sea

Neion /nī' ŏn/ A mountain on Ithaka

Kalypso /kə lĭp' sō/ A goddess who detains Odysseus seven years

Kirke /kûr' kē/ A sorceress who turns some of Odysseus' men into swine

Aiaia /ī ī′ ə/ The island where Kirke lives

Zeus /zūs/ The king of the gods

Euanthes /yū ăn′ thēz/ The father of Maron

Maron /mär′ ən/ A priest of Apollo who gives Odysseus gifts of gold and silver and strong liquor

Apollo /ə pŏl′ ō/ The god of music and poetry

Ismaros /ĭs′ mə rəs/ Odysseus' first stop after leaving Troy

Akhaians /ə kī′ ənz/ Inhabitants of Akhaia, a region in Greece

Agamemnon /ăg ə mĕm′ nŏn/ The commander-in-chief of the Greek armies in the Trojan War

Atreus /ā′ trē əs/ The father of Agamemnon

Athena /ə thē′ nə/ The goddess of wisdom, who befriends Odysseus

Poseidon /pō sī′ dən/ The god of the sea and of earthquakes

Telemos /tĕl′ ə məs/ A wizard who prophesied the blinding of Polyphemos by Odysseus

Eurymos /yûr′ ĭ məs/ The father of Telemos

ODYSSEUS AND THE KYKLOPS
From Book Nine of Homer's *Odyssey*

ROBERT FITZGERALD, TRANSLATOR

SPEAKERS

(Odysseus 1 tells the story. Odysseus 2 speaks the dialogue within the story.)

ODYSSEUS 1	**POLYPHEMOS**	**SAILOR 2**
CHORUS	**KYKLOPES**	**SAILOR 3**
ODYSSEUS 2	**SAILOR 1**	**SAILOR 4**
CREWMEN		

ODYSSEUS 1

Alkinoos, king and admiration of men,
how beautiful this is, to hear a minstrel
gifted as yours: a god he might be, singing!

There is no boon in life more sweet, I say,
than when a summer joy holds all the realm,
and banqueters sit listening to a harper
in great hall, by rows of tables heaped
with bread and roast meat, while a steward goes
to dip up wine and brim your cups again.
Here is the flower of life, it seems to me!
But now you wish to know my cause for sorrow—
and thereby give me cause for more.

What shall I
say first? What shall I keep until the end?
The gods have tried me in a thousand ways.
But first my name: let that be known to you,
and if I pull away from pitiless death,
friendship will bind us, though my land lies far.
I am Laertes' son, Odysseus. Men hold me
formidable for guile in peace and war:
this fame has gone abroad to the sky's rim.
My home is on the peaked sea-mark of Ithaka
under Mount Neion's wind-blown robe of leaves, . . .
a rocky isle, but good for a boy's training;
I shall not see on earth a place more dear,
though I have been detained long by Kalypso,
loveliest among goddesses, who held me
in her smooth caves, to be her heart's delight,
as Kirke of Aiaia, the enchantress,
desired me, and detained me in her hall.
But in my heart I never gave consent.
Where shall a man find sweetness to surpass
his own home and his parents? In far lands
he shall not, though he find a house of gold.

What of my sailing, then, from Troy? What of those
        years
of rough adventure, weathered under Zeus? . . .

ODYSSEUS 1 AND CHORUS

In [one] land we found were Kyklopes,
giants, louts, without a law to bless them.
In ignorance leaving the fruitage of the earth in
      mystery
to the immortal gods, they neither plow
nor sow by hand, nor till the ground, though grain—
wild wheat and barley—grows untended, and
wine-grapes, in clusters, ripen in heaven's rain.
Kyklopes have no muster[1] and no meeting,
no consultation or old tribal ways,
but each one dwells in his own mountain cave
dealing out rough justice to wife and child,
indifferent to what the others do.

ODYSSEUS 1

Well, then:
across the wide bay from the mainland
there lies a desert island, not far out,
but still not close inshore. . . .
Here we made harbor. Some god guided us
that night, for we could barely see our bows
in the dense fog around us, and no moonlight
filtered through the overcast. No look-out,
nobody saw the island dead ahead,
nor even the great landward rolling billow
that took us in: we found ourselves in shallows,
keels grazing shore: so furled our sails
and disembarked where the low ripples broke.
There on the beach we lay, and slept till morning. . . .

When the young Dawn with finger tips of rose
came in the east, I called my men together
and made a speech to them:

ODYSSEUS 2

Old shipmates, friends,
the rest of you stand by; I'll make the crossing
in my own ship, with my own company,
and find out what the mainland natives are—
for they may be wild savages, and lawless,
or hospitable and god-fearing men.

ODYSSEUS 1

At this I went aboard, and gave the word
to cast off by the stern. My oarsmen followed,
filing in to their benches by the rowlocks,
and all in line dipped oars in the grey sea.

ODYSSEUS 1 AND CHORUS

As we rowed on, and nearer to the mainland,
at one end of the bay, we saw a cavern
yawning above the water, screened with laurel,
and many rams and goats about the place
inside a sheepfold—made from slabs of stone
earthfast between tall trunks of pine and rugged
towering oak trees. A prodigious² man
slept in this cave alone, and took his flocks
to graze afield—remote from all companions,
knowing none but savage ways, a brute
so huge, he seemed no man at all of those
who eat good wheaten bread; but he seemed rather
a shaggy mountain reared in solitude.

ODYSSEUS 1

We beached there, and I told the crew
to stand by and keep watch over the ship;
as for myself I took my twelve best fighters
and went ahead. I had a goatskin full
of that sweet liquor that Euanthes' son,
Maron, had given me. He kept Apollo's

96

holy grove at Ismaros; for kindness
we showed him there, and showed his wife and child,
he gave me seven shining golden talents[3]
perfectly formed, a solid silver winebowl,
and then this liquor—twelve two-handled jars
of brandy, pure and fiery. . . . A wineskin full
I brought along, and victuals in a bag,
for in my bones I knew some towering brute
would be upon us soon—all outward power,
a wild man, ignorant of civility.

ODYSSEUS 1 AND CHORUS

We climbed, then, briskly to the cave. But Kyklops
had gone afield, to pasture his fat sheep,
so we looked round at everything inside:
a drying rack that sagged with cheeses, pens
crowded with lambs and kids, each in its class:
firstlings apart from middlings, and the 'dewdrops,'
or newborn lambkins, penned apart from both.
And vessels full of whey[4] were brimming there—
bowls of earthenware and pails for milking.

ODYSSEUS 1

My men came pressing round me, pleading:

CREWMEN

Why not take these cheeses, get them stowed, come
    back,
throw open all the pens, and make a run for it?
We'll drive the kids and lambs aboard. We say
put out again on good salt water!

ODYSSEUS 1

Ah, how sound that was! Yet I refused. I wished
to see the caveman, what he had to offer—
no pretty sight, it turned out, for my friends.

We lit a fire, burnt an offering,
and took some cheese to eat; then sat in silence
around the embers, waiting. When he came
he had a load of dry boughs on his shoulder
to stoke his fire at suppertime. He dumped it
with a great crash into that hollow cave,
and we all scattered fast to the far wall.
Then over the broad cavern floor he ushered
the ewes he meant to milk. He left his rams
and he-goats in the yard outside, and swung
high overhead a slab of solid rock
to close the cave. Two dozen four-wheeled wagons,
with heaving wagon teams, could not have stirred
the tonnage of that rock from where he wedged it
over the doorsill. Next he took his seat
and milked his bleating ewes. A practiced job
he made of it, giving each ewe her suckling;
thickened his milk, then, into curds[5] and whey,
sieved out the curds to drip in withy baskets,[6]
and poured the whey to stand in bowls
cooling until he drank it for his supper.
When all these chores were done, he poked the fire,
heaping on brushwood. In the glare he saw us.

POLYPHEMOS

Strangers, . . . who are you? And where from?
What brings you here by sea ways—a fair traffic?[7]
Or are you wandering rogues, who cast your lives
like dice, and ravage other folk by sea?

ODYSSEUS 1

We felt a pressure on our hearts, in dread
of that deep rumble and that mighty man.
But all the same I spoke up in reply:

ODYSSEUS 2

We are from Troy, Akhaians, blown off course
by shifting gales on the Great South Sea;
homeward bound, but taking routes and ways
uncommon; so the will of Zeus would have it.
We served under Agamemnon, son of Atreus—
the whole world knows what city
he laid waste, what armies he destroyed.
It was our luck to come here; here we stand,
beholden for your help, or any gifts
you give—as custom is to honor strangers.
We would entreat you, great Sir, have a care
for the gods' courtesy; Zeus will avenge
the unoffending guest.

ODYSSEUS 1

He answered this from his brute chest, unmoved:

POLYPHEMOS

You are a ninny,
or else you come from the other end of nowhere,
telling me, mind the gods! We Kyklopes
care not a whistle for your thundering Zeus
or all the gods in bliss; we have more force by far.
I would not let you go for fear of Zeus—
you or your friends—unless I had a whim to.
Tell me, where was it, now, you left your ship—
around the point, or down the shore, I wonder?

ODYSSEUS 1

He thought he'd find out, but I saw through this,
and answered with a ready lie:

ODYSSEUS 2

My ship? Poseidon Lord, who sets the earth a-tremble,
broke it up on the rocks at your land's end.

A wind from seaward served him, drove us there.
We are survivors, these good men and I.

ODYSSEUS 1

Neither reply nor pity came from him,
but in one stride he clutched at my companions
and caught two in his hands like squirming puppies
to beat their brains out, spattering the floor.
Then he dismembered them and made his meal,
gaping and crunching like a mountain lion—
everything: innards, flesh, and marrow bones.

ODYSSEUS 1 AND CHORUS

We cried aloud, lifting our hands to Zeus,
powerless, looking on at this, appalled;
but Kyklops went on filling his belly
with manflesh and great gulps of whey,
then lay down like a mast among his sheep.

ODYSSEUS 1

My heart beat high now at the chance of action,
and drawing the sharp sword from my hip I went
along his flank to stab him where the midriff
holds the liver. I had touched the spot
when sudden fear stayed me: if I killed him
we perished there as well, for we could never
move his ponderous doorway slab aside.
So we were left to groan and wait for morning.

ODYSSEUS 1 AND CHORUS

When the young Dawn with finger tips of rose
lit up the world, the Kyklops built a fire
and milked his handsome ewes, all in due order,
putting the sucklings to the mothers. Then,
his chores being all dispatched, he caught
another brace[8] of men to make his breakfast,

and whisked away his great door slab
to let his sheep go through—but he, behind,
reset the stone as one would cap a quiver.[9]
There was a din of whistling as the Kyklops
rounded his flock to higher ground, then stillness.

ODYSSEUS 1

And now I pondered how to hurt him worst,
if but Athena granted what I prayed for.
Here are the means I thought would serve my turn:
a club, or staff, lay there along the fold—
an olive tree, felled green and left to season
for Kyklops' hand. And it was like a mast
a lugger of twenty oars, broad in the beam—
a deep-sea-going craft—might carry:
so long, so big around, it seemed. Now I
chopped out a six-foot section of this pole
and set it down before my men, who scraped it;
and when they had it smooth, I hewed again
to make a stake with pointed end. I held this
in the fire's heart and turned it, toughening it,
then hid it, well back in the cavern, under
one of the dung piles in profusion there.
Now came the time to toss for it: who ventured
along with me? whose hand could bear to thrust
and grind that spike in Kyklops' eye, when mild
sleep had mastered him? As luck would have it,
the men I would have chosen won the toss—
four strong men, and I made five as captain.

ODYSSEUS 1 AND CHORUS

At evening came the shepherd with his flock,
his woolly flock. The rams as well, this time,
entered the cave: by some sheep-herding whim—
or a god's bidding—none were left outside.
He hefted his great boulder into place

and sat him down to milk the bleating ewes
in proper order, put the lambs to suck,
and swiftly ran through all his evening chores.
Then he caught two more men and feasted on them.

ODYSSEUS 1

My moment was at hand, and I went forward
holding an ivy bowl of my dark drink,
looking up, saying:

ODYSSEUS 2

Kyklops, try some wine.
Here's liquor to wash down your scraps of men.
Taste it, and see the kind of drink we carried
under our planks. I meant it for an offering
if you would help us home. But you are mad,
unbearable, a bloody monster! After this,
will any other traveler come to see you?

ODYSSEUS 1

He seized and drained the bowl, and it went down
so fiery and smooth he called for more:

POLYPHEMOS

Give me another, thank you kindly. Tell me,
how are you called? I'll make a gift will please you.
Even Kyklopes know the wine-grapes grow
out of grassland and loam in heaven's rain,
but here's a bit of nectar and ambrosia![10]

ODYSSEUS 1

Three bowls I brought him, and he poured them down.
I saw the fuddle and flush come over him,
then I sang out in cordial tones:

ODYSSEUS 2

Kyklops, you ask my honorable name? Remember

the gift you promised me, and I shall tell you.
My name is Nohbdy: mother, father, and friends,
everyone calls me Nohbdy.

ODYSSEUS 1

And he said:

POLYPHEMOS

Nohbdy's my meat, then, after I eat his friends.
Others come first. There's a noble gift, now.

ODYSSEUS 1 AND CHORUS

Even as he spoke, he reeled and tumbled backward,
his great head lolling to one side; and sleep
took him like any creature. Drunk, hiccuping,
he dribbled streams of liquor and bits of men.

ODYSSEUS 1

Now, by the gods, I drove my big hand spike
deep in the embers, charring it again,
and cheered my men along with battle talk
to keep their courage up: no quitting now.
The pike of olive, green though it had been,
reddened and glowed as if about to catch.
I drew it from the coals and my four fellows
gave me a hand, lugging it near the Kyklops
as more than natural force nerved them; straight
forward they sprinted, lifted it, and rammed it
deep in his crater eye, and I leaned on it
turning it as a shipwright turns a drill
in planking, having men below to swing
the two-handled strap that spins it in the groove.
So with our brand we bored that great eye socket
while blood ran out around the red hot bar.

ODYSSEUS 1 AND CHORUS

The Kyklops bellowed and the rock roared round him,

and we fell back in fear. Clawing his face
he tugged the bloody spike out of his eye,
threw it away, and his wild hands went groping;
then he set up a howl for Kyklopes
who lived in caves on windy peaks nearby.
Some heard him; and they came by divers ways
to clump around outside and call:

KYKLOPES

What ails you,
Polyphemos? Why do you cry so sore
in the starry night? You will not let us sleep.
Sure no man's driving off your flock? No man
has tricked you, ruined you?

ODYSSEUS 1

Out of the cave
the mammoth Polyphemos roared in answer:

POLYPHEMOS

Nohbdy, Nohbdy's tricked me, Nohbdy's ruined me!

ODYSSEUS 1

To this rough shout they made a sage reply:

KYKLOPES

Ah well, if nobody has played you foul
there in your lonely bed, we are no use in pain
given by great Zeus. Let it be your father,
Poseidon Lord, to whom you pray.

ODYSSEUS 1

So saying
they trailed away. And I was filled with laughter
to see how like a charm the name deceived them.
Now Kyklops, wheezing as the pain came on him,
fumbled to wrench away the great doorstone

and squatted in the breach with arms thrown wide
for any silly beast or man who bolted—
hoping somehow I might be such a fool.
But I kept thinking how to win the game:
death sat there huge; how could we slip away?
I drew on all my wits, and ran through tactics,
reasoning as a man will for dear life,
until a trick came—and it pleased me well.
The Kyklops' rams were handsome, fat, with heavy
fleeces, a dark violet. Three abreast
I tied them silently together, twining
cords of willow from the ogre's bed;
then slung a man under each middle one
to ride there safely, shielded left and right.
So three sheep could convey each man. I took
the woolliest ram, the choicest of the flock,
and hung myself under his kinky belly,
pulled up tight, with fingers twisted deep
in sheepskin ringlets for an iron grip.
So, breathing hard, we waited until morning.

ODYSSEUS 1 AND CHORUS

When Dawn spread out her finger tips of rose
the rams began to stir, moving for pasture,
and peals of bleating echoed round the pens
where dams with udders full called for a milking.

ODYSSEUS 1

Blinded, and sick with pain from his head wound,
the master stroked each ram, then let it pass,
but my men riding on the pectoral[11] fleece
the giant's blind hands blundering never found.
Last of them all my ram, the leader, came,
weighted by wool and me with my meditations.
The Kyklops patted him, and then he said:

105

POLYPHEMOS

Sweet cousin ram, why lag behind the rest
in the night cave? You never linger so,
but graze before them all, and go afar
to crop sweet grass, and take your stately way
leading along the streams, until at evening
you run to be the first one in the fold.
Why, now, so far behind? Can you be grieving
over your Master's eye? That carrion rogue
and his accurst companions burnt it out
when he had conquered all my wits with wine.
Nohbdy will not get out alive, I swear.
Oh, had you brain and voice to tell
where he may be now, dodging all my fury!
Bashed by this hand and bashed on this rock wall
his brains would strew the floor, and I should have
rest from the outrage Nohbdy worked upon me.

ODYSSEUS 1

He sent us into the open, then. Close by,
I dropped and rolled clear of the ram's belly,
going this way and that to untie the men.
With many glances back, we rounded up
his fat, stiff-legged sheep to take aboard,
and drove them down to where the good ship lay.
We saw, as we came near, our fellows' faces
shining; then we saw them turn to grief
tallying[12] those who had not fled from death.
I hushed them, jerking head and eyebrows up,
and in a low voice told them:

ODYSSEUS 2

Load this herd;
move fast, and put the ship's head toward the breakers.

ODYSSEUS 1

They all pitched in at loading, then embarked
and struck their oars into the sea. Far out,
as far off shore as shouted words would carry,
I sent a few back to the adversary:

ODYSSEUS 2

O Kyklops! Would you feast on my companions?
Puny, am I, in a Caveman's hands?
How do you like the beating that we gave you,
you cannibal? Eater of guests
under your roof! Zeus and the gods have paid you!

ODYSSEUS 1

The blind thing in his doubled fury broke
a hilltop in his hands and heaved it after us.
Ahead of our black prow it struck and sank
whelmed in a spuming geyser, a giant wave
that washed the ship stern foremost back to shore.
I got the longest boathook out and stood
fending us off, with furious nods to all
to put their backs into a racing stroke—
row, row, or perish. So the long oars bent
kicking the foam sternward, making head
until we drew away, and twice as far.
Now when I cupped my hands I heard the crew
in low voices protesting:

SAILOR 1

Godsake, Captain!
Why bait the beast again? Let him alone!

SAILOR 2

That tidal wave he made on the first throw
all but beached us.

SAILOR 3

All but stove[13] us in!

SAILOR 1

Give him our bearing with your trumpeting,
he'll get the range and lob a boulder.

SAILOR 4

Aye, he'll smash our timbers and our heads together!

ODYSSEUS 1

I would not heed them in my glorying spirit,
but let my anger flare and yelled:

ODYSSEUS 2

Kyklops, if ever mortal man inquire
how you were put to shame and blinded, tell him
Odysseus, raider of cities, took your eye:
Laertes' son, whose home's on Ithaka!

ODYSSEUS 1

At this he gave a mighty sob and rumbled:

POLYPHEMOS

Now comes the weird[14] upon me, spoken of old.
A wizard, grand and wondrous, lived here—Telemos,
a son of Eurymos; great length of days
he had in wizardry among the Kyklopes,
and these things he foretold for time to come:
my great eye lost, and at Odysseus' hands.
Always I had in mind some giant, armed
in giant force, would come against me here.
But this, but you—small, pitiful and twiggy—
you put me down with wine, you blinded me.
Come back, Odysseus, and I'll treat you well,
praying the god of earthquake to befriend you—
his son I am, for he by his avowal

fathered me, and, if he will, he may
heal me of this black wound—he and no other
of all the happy gods or mortal men.

ODYSSEUS 1

Few words I shouted in reply to him:

ODYSSEUS 2

If I could take your life I would and take
your time away, and hurl you down to hell!
The god of earthquake could not heal you there!

ODYSSEUS 1

At this he stretched his hands out in his darkness
toward the sky of stars, and prayed Poseidon:

POLYPHEMOS

O hear me, lord, blue girdler of the islands,
if I am thine indeed, and thou art father:
grant that Odysseus, raider of cities, never
see his home: Laertes' son, I mean,
who kept his hall on Ithaka. Should destiny
intend that he shall see his roof again
among his family in his father land,
far be that day, and dark the years between.
Let him lose all companions, and return
under strange sail to bitter days at home.

ODYSSEUS 1

In these words he prayed, and the god heard him.

[1] **muster:** assembly   [2] **prodigious:** enormous
[3] **talents:** pieces of gold used as money   [4] **whey:** the watery part of milk
[5] **curds:** coagulated solids in milk   [6] **withy baskets:** baskets made of vines or
slender twigs   [7] **traffic:** trade or business   [8] **brace:** pair
[9] **quiver:** a case for carrying arrows   [10] **ambrosia:** the food of the gods
[11] **pectoral:** on the chest   [12] **tallying:** counting up
[13] **stove:** crushed (the sides of the boat) inward   [14] **weird:** fate, doom

The story of "The Two Sisters" has been recited and sung since the days of the Vikings of northern Europe. It originated in Scandinavia, from where it traveled to Iceland, the British Isles, and North America. In this version, the two sisters live in Scotland, "by the bonny [fine] mill-dams of Binnorie." Custom requires that any man who wishes to marry into the family should propose to the elder sister first. Unfortunately, however, the knight who comes to woo prefers the younger girl.

THE TWO SISTERS OF BINNORIE

ANONYMOUS

SPEAKERS

NARRATOR	YOUNGEST SISTER
CHORUS	MILLER'S SON
ELDEST SISTER	HARP

NARRATOR

There were two sisters sat in a bower;

CHORUS

Binnorie, O Binnorie!

NARRATOR

There came a knight to be their wooer;

CHORUS

By the bonny mill-dams of Binnorie.

NARRATOR

He courted the eldest with gloves and rings,
But he loved the youngest above all things.
The eldest was vexed to despair,
And much she envied her sister fair.
The eldest said to the youngest one,

ELDEST SISTER

Will ye see our father's ships come in?

NARRATOR

She's taken her by the lily-white hand,
And led her down to the river strand.
The youngest stood upon a stone;
The eldest came and pushed her in.

YOUNGEST SISTER

O sister, sister, reach your hand,
And you shall be heir of half my land.
O sister, reach me but your glove
And sweet William shall be all your love.

ELDEST SISTER

Sink on, nor hope for hand or glove!
Sweet William shall surely be my love.

NARRATOR

Sometimes she sank, sometimes she swam,
Until she came to the mouth of the dam.
Out then came the miller's son
And saw the fair maid swimming in.

MILLER'S SON

O father, father, draw your dam!
Here's either a mermaid or a swan.

NARRATOR

The miller hasted and drew his dam,
And there he found a drowned woman.

CHORUS

You could not see her middle small,
Her girdle was so rich withal.

You could not see her yellow hair
For the gold and pearls that clustered there.

NARRATOR

And by there came a harper fine,
Who harped to nobles when they dine.
And when he looked that lady on,
He sighed and made a heavy moan.
He's taken three locks of her yellow hair
And with them strung his harp so rare.
He went into her father's hall
To play his harp before them all.
But as he laid it on a stone,
The harp began to play alone.
And soon the harp sang loud and clear:

HARP

Farewell, my father and mother dear,
Farewell, farewell, my brother Hugh,
Farewell, my William, sweet and true.

NARRATOR

And then as plain as plain could be,

CHORUS

Binnorie, O Binnorie!

HARP

There sits my sister who drownèd me

CHORUS

By the bonny mill-dams of Binnorie!